# How to Live with the Stars

## QUEST BOOKS

are published by The Theosophical
Society in America, a branch of
a world organization dedicated to the
promotion of brotherhood and the
encouragement of the study of religion,
philosophy, and science, to the end
that man may better understand
himself and his place in the universe.
The Society stands for complete
freedom of individual search and belief.
Quest Books are offered as a
contribution to man's search for truth.

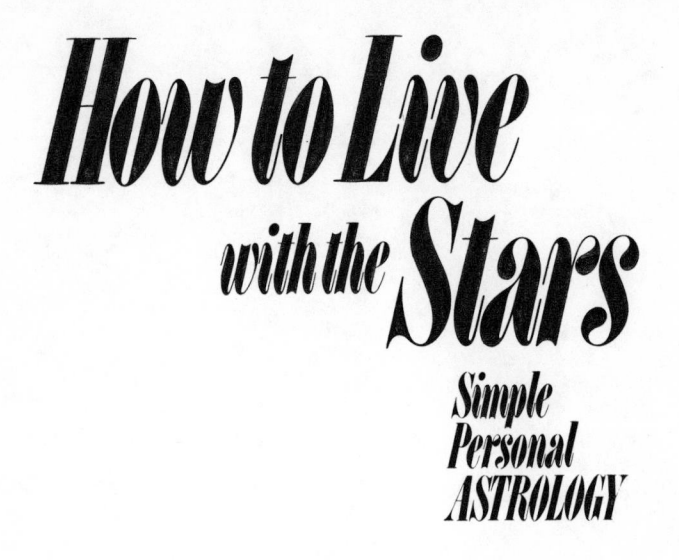

# How to Live with the Stars

## with the Stars

### Simple Personal ASTROLOGY

by

# MARC EDMUND JONES

A QUEST BOOK

THE THEOSOPHICAL PUBLISHING HOUSE
Wheaton, Ill., U.S.A.
Madras, India / London, England

A Quest original. First edition, 1976, published
by the Theosophical Publishing House, Wheaton,
Illinois, a department of the Theosophical Society
in America.

Library of Congress Cataloging in Publication Data

Jones, Marc Edmund, 1888-
    How to live with the stars.

    (A Quest book)
    Includes index.
    1. Astrology.  I. Title.
BF1708.1.J67     133.5     75-32401
ISBN 0-8356-0476-4
ISBN 0-8356-0473-X pbk.

Printed in the United States of America

# TABLE OF CONTENTS
# PART I
## PERSONAL ASTROLOGY BY
## ZODIACAL SIGNS ALONE

# PART II
## PERSONAL ASTROLOGY BY
## USE OF AN EPHEMERIS

# PART III
## PERSONAL ASTROLOGY BY
## USE OF A HOROSCOPE

# PART IV

## PRACTICAL APPLICATION

# ILLUSTRATIONS

## Charts and Tables

This book is dedicated to the devotees of a personal astrology, where the concern is the special problem of the individual in his adjustment to the more serious potentials of his life. It is not particularly concerned with the ebb and flow of everyday circumstances. They will go their largely superficial course, with man able to do very little about them.

# PART I

## *PERSONAL ASTROLOGY BY ZODIACAL SIGNS ALONE*

# INTRODUCTION
## *PLANETS AND ZODIAC*

When an individual wholly unfamiliar with the horoscope and astrological procedures of any sort, but who
becomes curious about all this or seeks the help of astrology,
there are only two things he can do. He can get in touch with
an astrologer, or he can find some way to become informed
to whatever extent he wishes. The present pages are de-
signed to meet the need in the latter case, and they are
prepared for use in progressive stages of possible interest.

Thus (1) at the start, no prior acquaintance of any sort
with the horoscopic technicalities is demanded. The reader
is introduced to the slower moving planets, and told what
their heavenly positions will mean at any particular time
now or ahead for a while. Then (2) for consideration of
other planets that travel through the heavens too swiftly for
such general identification, he is introduced to easily available tables of their current places in the zodiac. He thus can
find out what the astrological significance of the faster ones
may be for him. He now begins to know a little of the
language and systems of notation employed in astrology.
He must be able to recognize the common symbols of the
ten planets used by astrologers, as well as of the twelve signs
or segments into which the zodiac is divided. Here is the
total of twenty-two symbols he must know in order to use
the tables in the astrological ephemeris. He still is under no
necessity to have any more detailed grasp of astrology, to
make full and fruitful use of this simplified manual thus
far. Only (3) with the later and final stage in its pages will he
need to familiarize himself with the common form of a
horoscope. That he can be helped to do, in due course, if he
desires to plunge more deeply into horoscopic interpretation.

At this stage however he may gain a great deal of help
from everyday life in these modern times. The twelve signs
of the zodiac, from Aries through Pisces, are more and

more a matter of interest to the general public. Nearly everybody knows his birth sign, or where the sun was in the zodiac on the day he was born. People usually know something about most of the ten planets commonly employed in astrology. This number includes the sun, taken conveniently as a planet in horoscopic perspective, as well as the moon which of course is actually a satellite of the earth. Of the other eight, the ones nearest the sun in their orbits are seen frequently in the skies. These are Venus and Jupiter most spectacularly, and to lesser extent Mars and Saturn and perhaps Mercury. Reference to the planets, and to the pagan gods after which they were named, is commonplace in literature. Other symbolism throughout astronomical and astrological writings has similar common roots, and can become equally well-known very quickly.

## TABLE A
## THE BASIC SYMBOLS

| *Signs* | | *Planets* | |
|---------|---|-----------|---|
| Aries | ♈ | The Sun | ☉ |
| Taurus | ♉ | The moon | ☽ |
| Gemini | ♊ | Mercury | ☿ |
| Cancer | ♋ | Venus | ♀ |
| Leo | ♌ | Mars | ♂ |
| Virgo | ♍ | Jupiter | ♃ |
| Libra | ♎ | Saturn | ♄ |
| Scorpio | ♏ | Uranus | ♅ |
| Sagittarius | ♐ | Neptune | ♆ |
| Capricorn | ♑ | Pluto | ♇ |
| Aquarius | ♒ | | |
| Pisces | ♓ | | |

## *ASTROLOGICAL THEORY*

It may seem quite scientific to believe that there are intelligent cosmic forces that can pick out John Doe to endow him with a sudden fortune, and to consign Richard Roe to years of torture with terminal cancer, but life is not and never has been that simple. The horoscope does give remarkable testimony to vital details in the drama of individuality, but never a matter of fatalistic certainty such as can be ferreted out long in advance by those clever enough to perform the feat. The issue is not a lack of adequate skill, to account for the continual failures to do this successfully, but rather the need for a better understanding. A proper question is, "What is astrology all about, anyhow?" Answers of various sorts are a dime a dozen. Nonetheless it must be realized that (1) all human existence takes place in an extraordinary complex, and ultimately very mysterious, universe stretching away to infinity in every direction, and that (2) every living individual in very similar, if infinitely smaller, fashion is no less a different and altogether baffling universe in any way of thinking about it. Who has ever really plumbed the depths of his quite distinctive and private existence? Here is a conception of the big and the little that forever are mirroring each other in many ways.

This is by far the oldest known astrological idea, and it has had lasting influence upon human thought. It may have originated in ancient Mesopotamia. It had early parallel, if perhaps vaguely, in China and elsewhere. It fundamentally was the basis of alchemy, and in due course it developed into the art of the horoscope and individual character analysis. Aside from astrology, there came to be very broad philosophical recognition of the macrocosm—or the greater universe of all things—existing in an unceasing balance with the microcosm—or smaller universe of each different human being—in every special case. This "as above so below" conception was developed at least prior to Socrates, and it reached its peak of influence with such important philosophers of the Renaissance as Paracelsus. In recent times it has been a key principle in a modern and popular occultism. Each of the myriad upon myriad of microcosms of every sort is seen contributing in some fashion to the one macrocosm in its endless manifestation of itself, and by the same token (and reciprocally) each one of them must at the same time be helped to exist in its necessary individual uniqueness.

When it came to any sort of total view of this wonderful world in which all existence found itself, ancient man must have seen its reality reflected in the shifting face of the heavens perhaps more than anywhere else. The daily revolution of the celestial sphere with its establishment of day and night would be a beginning, but more challenging to the mind might well be the seasonal differences of summer and winter marked off by the annual circuit of the fixed stars in the permanent patterns they had established in the sky. And then there would be the endless modifications of these groupings by what were earlier known as the moveable stars, or what now are recognized as planets of the solar system. Dramatically visible to the eye, they kept changing place continually in a way quite likely to have suggested orderliness of some sort. This dependable regularity of change could easily have seemed a clue to a worldly reality. Of course far earlier the rapid shift of the moon with its phases, would have been found to have correlation with the ocean tides and the planting and growth of plants and possible breeding of animals. Certainly this indicated something more than mere haphazard everyday existence.

The zodiac, or arrangement in the earth's perspective of the fixed stars in a narrow band around the heavens in thirty-degree constellations, has remained unchanged for five thousand years or more. The word zodiac is from the Greek, and it means the glyphs for the creatures or figures used to identify these constellations. At about 450 B.C. they were systematized to facilitate astronomical computation, and Aries 0° was established permanently as the place of the sun at the vernal equinox. In the second century B.C. the Greek astronomer Hipparchus discovered the precession of the equinoxes, a third very slow movement of the earth in the heavens, although not noticeable like its daily rotation on its axis or its annual revolution around its orbit. Through precession, however, the zodiacal constellations in the last some twenty-five hundred years have each moved more than the full width of itself from any correspondence to the astrological signs, to which the original names have been transferred. With the creation of the horoscope, perhaps as early as the fifth century B.C., the equinoxes became important in determining zodiacal significance.

In the northern hemisphere the vernal—or spring—equinox, so very evident in correspondence to the seasonal quickening, is taken as the starting point for the zodiacal scheme. It is the cusp or threshold of the sign Aries, or 0° of celestial longitude. In the southern hemisphere the astrological nature of the equinoxes is reversed, but this is no real difficulty and it needs no attention in these pages. In respect to the proposition, of what astrology is all about, this is the end of the matter astronomically. No further connection with astronomy exists except for the dependence on that scientific discipline for the celestial data needed in horoscopic analysis.

## ASTROLOGICAL SIGNIFICANCE

As in all life and everyday reality, significance arises from experience. It is developed gradually, and with much adjustment and refinement before gaining any permanent form. Such obvious correlations of the moon's cycles with the tides in the ocean, or with the biological rhythm of man's organic structure, are only a start in astrological significance. Ultimately it is a vast spread of cosmic eccentricities of a sort that can be found significant in correspondence to known or observed human differentiations. All possible distinctions in the one overall universe must be recognized, or perhaps in a sense imagined, before in immensely long periods of trial and error they can be matched with any certainty in their delineation of the human individual's points of equivalent difference or exceptionality.

The foundational system of relationship through which the signs of the zodiac gain their astrological significance for man is established by (1) the equinoxes, or Aries at the spring or vernal point and Libra directly opposite at the balancing autumnal one and (2) the extremes of lean away from each other of the earth's great zodiacal and equatorial circles in the heavens at the corresponding solstice points, which mark off the equally distinctive seasons of summer and winter or Cancer and Capricorn respectively. These four zodiacal signs comprise the astrologer's basic quadrature.

Aries, Cancer, Libra and Capricorn are known as CARDINAL by quadrature. Together they have been found to identify a characteristic immediateness of significance, or an individual sort of functioning that always is at the ready in one way or another. Revealed is an instinctive attunement to any possibility of change or adjustment, as well as a characteristic directness of response to all potentials of the moment. Here is one phase of human functioning through which experience is continually brought to its living actuality.

As the zodiac rises regularly at the horizon in the east the four zodiacal signs seen just ahead of each of the CARDINAL ones and in a way preparing the way for it, are known as COMMON in their quadrature functioning. Pisces, Gemini, Virgo and Sagittarius delineate a trait of individuality that operates best in a serving sort of way. They reveal personal availability that frequently becomes a marked self-dedication to some special phase of everyday living. To see Pisces as preparing the ground for Aries, Gemini for Cancer, Virgo for Libra and Sagittarius for Capricorn in the symbolism is primarily to gain a deeper insight into the underlying nature of quadrature distinction. But COMMON emphasis is never in any possible way a limiting or modification of man's CARDINAL potentiality. Thus a hand can do what it is doing irrespective of what a foot is doing or is able to do on its own, and yet in larger perspective the hand can be of either assistance or handicap to the foot's action.

It must indeed be remembered that nobody is ever a pure manifestation of a single sign of the zodiac, but is always, and to highly varying extent, a representation of all of them. The high genius of astrological delineations is its charting of the underlying traits, that make up the total individuality, in an effective one-at-a-time fashion. This can lead to the solution of problems through a convenient few of the personal traits that may be most responsible for the particular problem.

The four zodiacal signs directly following the CARDINAL ones as the zodiac rises in the east, or those which in a sense delineate the fundamentally established consequences of the human experience that has been or now can be brought to living actuality, are known as FIXED. They identify a trait of individuality that operates in the learning of lessons in life, or its ordering on the basis of an intelligibility whether gained personally or accepted by instinct or reason. This is the realm of norms and values that are the conscious side of all human functioning. To see Aries in a sense certified through Taurus, Cancer through Leo, Libra through Scorpio and Capricorn through Aquarius in the underlying symbolization is primarily to achieve a more effective understanding of the continuities of everyday reality, and thus to gain a greater power of imagination and psychological elbowroom in all truly conscious existence. This is viewing man as a whole while helping him through an analysis of the parts, each part in its own special genius.

## THE QUADRATURES

Of equal importance with the quadratures, in establishing the structure of the zodiac and its twelve signs, are the triplicities. To understand their indication it might be helpful to visualize the common wheelbarrow, by which materials can be moved about with an appreciable conservation of energy or strain. Two hands can operate well apart to lift up any given load, and with single-wheel support take it through or around obstacles or over irregular surfaces. Symbolically a significant point on a circle can find a functional effectiveness by triangular relationship with two related points, each a third of the circle away from it in opposite directions, and these two linked with each other by the remaining third of the circle. Thus the three points create a symmetry that in symbolism is momentum, as a continual or possible progress in some special fashion. It can operate at any or all three points.

# THE QUADRATURES

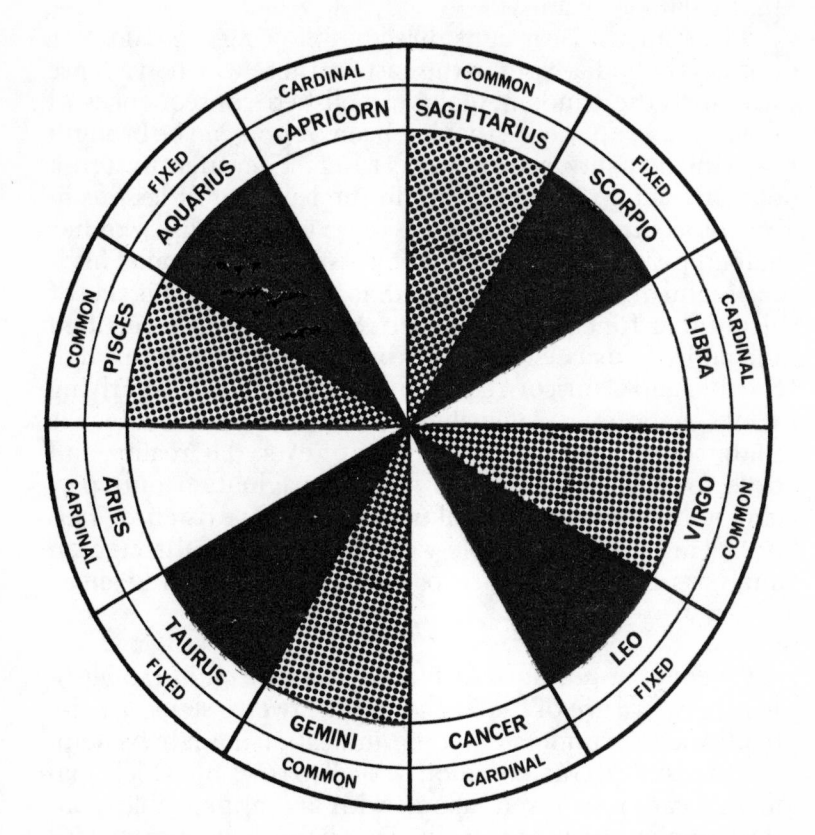

Inscribing the equal-sided triangle in the circle can actually be an initial step in establishing a series of such regular polygons inscribed in the circle with the number of their sides increased one by one, until in a sense a final one of them becomes the circle. It thereupon symbolizes perfection or fullness of some kind, of which the triangle is the first or original promise. Indeed, in almost universal acceptance, the triangle and the circle have both come to represent higher or spiritual and perhaps very magical potential.

In astrology the triangle in consequence always has an essentially transcendental intimation. Thus a zodiacal sign gains dimension when its own quadrature is linked in co-operation with each of the other quadratures in triangular rather than mere adjacent relationship. This is the genesis of horoscopic triplicity. The astrologer considers Aries-Leo-Sagittarius as of greater overall or more transcendental implication than the more casual Pisces-Aries-Taurus interrelation that has been pointed out. Just how and when these triplicities came to be associated with the supposedly four basic elements of the cosmos, identified by early natural philosophers, is beyond all reconstruction today. Fire, water, air and earth are hardly cognate terms. How flaming, liquidity, gaseousness, and solidity could be the universal building blocks is a very real puzzle. However, as late as the seventeenth century, two German chemists advanced the theory of phlogiston or a possible necessary element in the phenomenon of burning in parallel with the lines of alchemical speculation. In any case mankind is far from having all the answers, and there may be an elusive insight here that could prove most enlightening if ever understood. In the meanwhile astrology has accepted these names, and has built its own meanings into them over long generations. Their implications are valid because the unquestionable source has been actual human experience.

## THE TRIPLICITIES

The astrological element of FIRE is brought to most simple focus in the zodiac at the vernal equinox. It represents the potentiality of pure origin in existence and experience. This is paralleled in human reality by the springtime of any or all functioning. Here is emphasis of unconditioned individualism in its capacity to project itself out of itself in any manner, or under virtually any conditions whatsoever. This fundamentally is the urge to be or to live, as taking first positive rank in the makeup of anything that has distinctive

identification in the complexities with which it may be involved at any moment. It is close in practical manifestation
to what can be an almost complete self-sufficiency.

## THE TRIPLICITIES

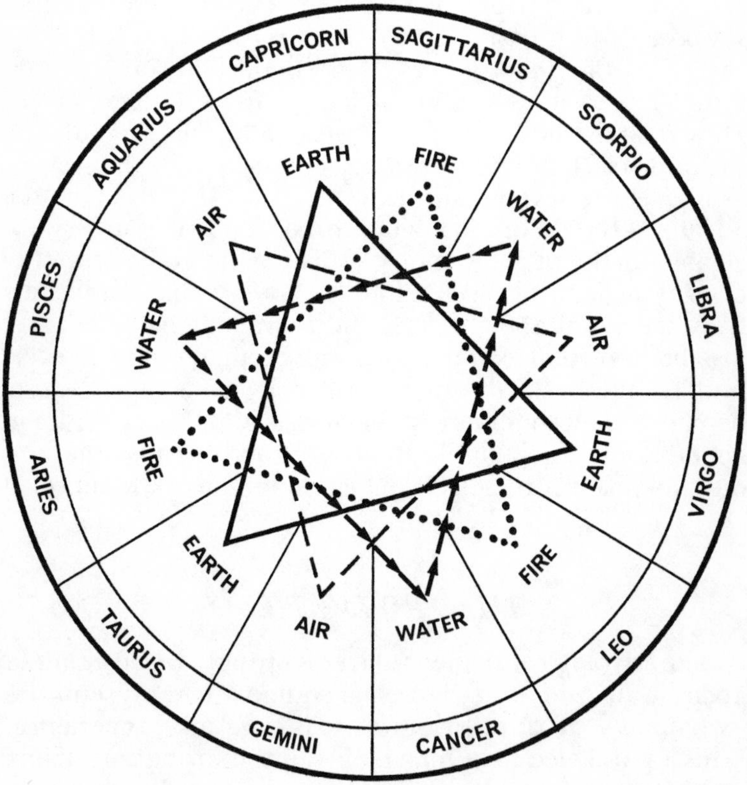

The balancing astrological element of AIR is brought to most simple focus in the zodiac at the autumnal equinox. It represents the potentiality of an entirely free exploitation of individual distinctiveness in existence and experience. This is paralleled in human reality by the harvest-time of any and all functioning. Here is emphasis of selfhood in its capacity to prove or justify itself through its selectivity, or conscious direction of its originating genius in even the least of things. This fundamentally is the drift through eventuations as a continual and ingenuous self-employment of personal identity. It is close in practical manifestation to what can be an ever-building pride in accomplishment.

The astrological element of WATER is brought to most simple focus in the zodiac at the summer solstice. It represents the potentiality of pure containment in existence and experience. This is paralleled in human reality by the mid-summer of any and all functioning. Here is emphasis of unconditioned comprehensiveness in its capacity to draw virtually anything or everything of any sort into the very substance of selfhood. This, fundamentally, is the appetite for a complete psychological embrace of whatever may be discerned in everyday ongoing, as taking first negative rank in the makeup of the conscious entity at any moment of attention. It is close in practical manifestation to an infinitely extended voraciousness.

The balancing astrological element of EARTH is brought to most simple focus in the zodiac at the winter solstice. It represents the potentiality of totally unfettered involvement in the interweaving details of existence and experience. This is paralleled in human reality by the wintertime of any and all functioning. Here is emphasis of pure assiduousness or capacity, as compensation for the bleak gestative time of Mother Nature, of man's increasing executive consummations in personal practicality. This fundamentally is the affinity for everything of possible or ultimate significance, such as can somehow be brought to some evidence of its promise and so shaped to its genuine ends. It is close in practical manifestation to an ever-building pride in special competence.

# ZODIACAL CLASSIFICATION

## *Quadratures*

| Cardinal | ♈ ♋ ♎ ♑ | Immediateness |
| Fixed | ♉ ♌ ♍ ♒ | Intelligibility |
| Common | ♊ ♏ ♐ ♓ | Availability |

## *Triplicities*

| Fire | ♈ ♌ ♐ | Individualism |
| Earth | ♉ ♍ ♑ | Assiduousness |
| Air | ♊ ♎ ♒ | Selectivity |
| Water | ♋ ♏ ♓ | Comprehensiveness |

## ASTROLOGICAL KEYWORDS

The greatest problem in astrological interpretation is that the real meaning of an indication in actual experience is as much determined by the performance of an individual as by its potentiality that the planets and other horoscopic factors reveal. A true astrology shows possibilities, and it shows them impartially. Thus it adjusts to the use made of them, and in consequence it cannot do this too literally in advance. A very valuable analytical procedure, to help hold to this impartiality and essentially liquid realization seems to have been pioneered by Max Heindel. Later it was popularized by Manly Palmer Hall. This is the method of keywords.

The trouble with most everyday language is that words gain color and become imprecise. Thus courage can be foolhardiness or steadiness under pressure, and ambition can be aggressiveness or a laudable pursuit of goals. Therefore less common words have to be selected to take on a technical exactness that can be learned precisely, and so contribute to clear thinking. This is seen in all the sciences and areas of disciplined analysis. It can degenerate into a jargon, as all language can become slang, but it is the way in which mental competence best protects itself. The astrological quadratures and triplicities have presented an example of keywords, and in the formulas of delineation of these pages they will be indicated by small capitals as already have been done with CARDINAL and FIRE and so on.

# CHAPTER ONE

# *THE NATURE OF THE SIGNS*

ARIES charts the astrological function of a CARDINAL immediateness with the individualism delineated by the zodiacal element of FIRE, and establishes the keyword ASPIRATION. Here, in the overall pattern of the world at large, is the forward urge of the masses represented in the very familiar determination of anything alive to stay alive or strengthen its security. In the particular instance the effort may be to contribute to the welfare of everyone else in order to further this. The underlying manifestation of this general phase of conscious, or instinctive, existence is an egocentricity that, at worst, can be ruthless arrogance but, at best, a well-balance disposition. The symbol adopted for this manner of activity by the ancient astrologers, and still in universal use, is the ram or male sheep. The graphic representation is apparently his two horns.

TAURUS charts the astrological function of a FIXED intelligibility with the assiduousness delineated by the zodiacal element of EARTH and establishes the keyword VIRILITY. Here, in the overall pattern of the world at large, is the affinity of the masses for the development and exercise and display of human prowess, or the testing of selfhood through some dominance over natural realities or other people at crucial moments. In the particular instance the attempt may be to accomplish given ends by exaggerated self-expenditure. The underlying manifestation of this general phase of conscious, or instinctive, existence is a self-confidence that, at worst, can be destructively unsocial but, at best, an exceptional everyday competence. The symbol adopted for this manner of action by the ancient astrologers, and still in universal use, is the bull. The graphic representation is apparently his face and horns.

GEMINI charts the astrological function of a COMMON availability with the selectivity delineated by the zodiacal element of AIR, and establishes the keyword VIVIFICATION. Here, in the overall pattern of the world at large, is the spontaneous drift of the masses to freewheeling experimentation whenever eventuation or situation comes to any issue, or the wide-ranging extemporization that is at the core of all human progress. In the particular instance the effort may be to stimulate anything of self through a fresh recognition of relevancies or exaggerated employment of significance. The underlying manifestation of this general phase of conscious, or instinctive, existence is a largely uninhibited activity that, at worst, can be callous exploitation of others but, at best, a priceless camaraderie. The symbol adopted for this manner of activity by the ancient astrologers, and still in universal use, is the twins. The graphic representation is merely two upright lines linked together.

CANCER charts the astrological function of a CARDINAL immediateness with the comprehensiveness delineated by the zodiacal element of WATER and establishes the keyword EXPANSION. Here, in the overall pattern of the world at large, is the appetite of the masses for definite, personal elbow-room, or for the ever-expanding selfhood that was the crucial factor of self-existence in childhood. In the particular instance the attempt may be to gain self-substantiation through every sort of quick and, even if transient, widening of horizons. The underlying manifestation of this general phase of conscious, or instinctive, existence is an insatiability that, at worst, is dangerous indulgence and, at best, an illimitable generosity. The symbol adopted for this manner of activity by the ancient astrologers, and still in universal use, is the crab. The graphic representation is apparently a pair of conventionalized claws.

LEO charts the astrological function of a FIXED intelligibility with the individualism delineated by the zodiacal element of FIRE, and establishes the keyword ASSURANCE. Here, in the overall pattern of the world at large, is the forward urge of the masses evident in the very familiar tendency of living things to establish themselves in definitive groups of some special kind, or to gain security in fellow competence. In the particular instance the effort may be to achieve self-distinction in order to maintain such an anchorage among others. The underlying manifestation of this general phase of conscious, or instinctive, an inescapable pride that, at worst, can be unscrupulous aggrandisement but, at best, a tireless accomplishment. The symbol adopted for this manner of activity by the ancient astrologers, and still in universal use, is the lion. The graphic representation is apparently the head and mane.

VIRGO charts the astrological function of a COMMON availability with the assiduousness delineated by the zodiacal element of EARTH, and establishes the keyword ASSIMILATION. Here, in the overall pattern of the world at large, is the affinity of the masses for the endless properties and even subtle resources of experience, or the basic substance of existence as something to be especially conserved. In the particular instance, the attempt may be to enlist all things in mutual service to each other. The underlying manifestation of this general phase of conscious, or instinctive, existence is a ramifying concern that, at worst, can be very destructive officiousness but, at best, an endless benefit to others. The symbol adopted for this manner of activity by the ancient astrologers, and still in universal use, is the virgin. The graphic representation is thought to be an "M" for primitive matter with an added stroke to suggest a chastity belt.

LIBRA charts the astrological function of a CARDINAL immediateness with the selectivity delineated by the zodiacal element of AIR, and establishes the keyword EQUIVALENCE. Here, in the overall pattern of the world at large, is the spontaneous drift of the masses marked by eager involvement in passing affairs, or the finding of possible pertinence in every eventuation of the moment. In the particular instance, the untiring effort may be to bring

effective challenging to personal experience. The underlying manifestation of this general phase of conscious, or
instinctive, an open-mindedness that, at worst, can be an
utterly insincere obsequiousness but, at best, a genuine
capacity for bringing others into harmony or effective
cooperation. The symbol adopted for this manner of activity by the ancient astrologers, and still in universal use, is the
balance or scales. The graphic representation is obviously a
conventionalized balance.

SCORPIO charts the astrological function of a FIXED intelligibility with the comprehensiveness delineated by the
zodiacal element of WATER, and establishes the keyword
CREATIVITY. Here, in the overall pattern of the world at
large, is the appetite of the masses for endlessly creative
self-expression, or an irresistible tendency to tinker with
everyday reality. In the particular instance the attempt may
be to achieve some imaginative transformation of almost
anything at all into some heightened significance. The
underlying manifestation of this general phase of conscious, or instinctive existence, is an unbridled self-
exploitation that, at worst, can be dangerously vindictive
but, at best, a stark therapeutic magic. The symbolism
adopted for this manner of action by the ancient astrologers, and still in universal use, is the scorpion although
there has been some effort to substitute the eagle. The
graphic representation is the "M" as perhaps representing
primitive matter and with the venomous tail of the insect
suggested by a pointed extra stroke.

SAGITTARIUS charts the astrological function of a
COMMON availability with the individualism delineated by
the zodiacal element of FIRE, and establishes the keyword
ADMINISTRATION Here, in the overall pattern of the world at
large, is the forward urge of the masses through their
inescapable gregariousness at core, or the tendency to find
shared compatibilities to enjoy in one way or another. In the
particular instance the effort may be to stake out special
interest in every avenue of personal advantage. The under-

lying manifestation of this general phase of conscious, or instinctive, existence is a fundamental, happy-go-lucky spirit that, at worst, can be cruel indifference to others but, at best, is a high gift for organizing everyday life to exceptionally practical advantage. The symbolism adopted for this manner of activity by the ancient astrologers, and still in universal use, is the centaur archer. The graphic representation is apparently a stylized arrow.

CAPRICORN charts the astrological function of a CARDINAL immediateness with assiduousness delineated by the zodiacal element of EARTH, and establishes the keyword DISCRIMINATION. Here, in the overall pattern of the world at large, is the affinity of the masses for law and order as they see it, or whatever they find that will protect the fruits of their everyday effort. In the particular instance the attempt may be to line up everything for personal convenience. The underlying manifestation of this general phase of conscious, or instinctive, existence is a fundamental criticism that, at worst, can be altogether disruptive but, at best, a continual and invaluable revaluation of life at every point of consideration. The symbolism adopted for this manner of activity by the ancient astrologers, and still in universal use, is the goat. The graphic symbol is a stylized head and horn, and this is slightly varied in some tables that use a different type face.

AQUARIUS charts the astrological function of a FIXED intelligibility with the selectivity delineated by the zodiacal element of AIR, and establishes the keyword LOYALTY. Here, in the overall pattern of the world at large, is the spontaneous drift of the masses in a natural tendency to cling to the familiar, and to accept either the necessity, or the value of their blind allegiance. In the particular instance the effort may be to find psychological support in people or causes at every point in life. The underlying manifestation of this general phase of conscious, or instinctive, a fundamental fixation that, at worst, can be a dangerous bigotry but, at best, an ability to develop a sort of spiritual charm in holding firm to what may be especially worthwhile in life's unfoldment. The symbolism adopted for this manner of activity by the ancient astrologers, and still in universal use, is the water-carrier. The graphic symbol is two zigzagging lines, perhaps in representation of waves spilled on the ground from a jar on the shoulder.

PISCES charts the astrological function of COMMON availability with the comprehensiveness delineated by the zodiacal element of WATER and establishes the keyword SYMPATHY. Here, in the overall pattern of the world at large, is the appetite of the masses for the intimacies of relationship possible for mankind, or the added enjoyment through sharing with others in both receiving and giving. In the particular instance the attempt may be to find private and privileged opportunities along this line. The underlying manifestation of this general phase of conscious, or instinctive, existence is the establishment of a very personal world that, at worst, can become complete delusion but, at best, can gestate great poetic or inspired realization for everybody. The symbolism adopted for this area of reality by the ancient astrologers, and still in universal use, is the fishes. The graphic symbol is two curved lines to represent them and a small stroke to show how they may be bound together and keep watch in opposite directions.

## TABLE C

## THE ZODIACAL KEYWORDS

| Aries | Aspiration | Libra | Equivalence |
|-------|------------|-------|-------------|
| Taurus | Virility | Scorpio | Creativity |
| Gemini | Vivification | Sagittarius | Administration |
| Cancer | Expansion | Capricorn | Discrimination |
| Leo | Assurance | Aquarius | Loyalty |
| Virgo | Assimilation | Pisces | Sympathy |

Chapter Two
## *PLANETARY INDICATION*

The entire basis of practical astrology is (1) the changes or shifts in position or activity of factors as observed from the earth in the celestial vault and, (2) the determination of suggestive correspondence of the heavenly phenomena to eventuations on the earth and in human experience. Modern horoscopy differs from its ancient counterpart in many ways in parallel with man's growth as the social creature, and perhaps most importantly in the adjustments that now have to be made in view of the entrance of mankind into the dawning great Aquarian Age. These major ages, or immense periods of history, correspond astrologically to the precession of the equinoxes through some particular zodiacal sign, comprising some twenty-two centuries at a time. Specific identification is of such a historical span, but there will be considerable overlapping of each into its next and this might well be different in various places around the globe. The phenomenon of precession was discovered by Hipparchus and, as already explained, the original constellations of the fixed stars were more decisively defined and their names taken to identify the zodiacal signs. The first degree of Aries might have been located precisely in the systematic mapping of the heavens around 450 B.C.

The movement in this precessional measure is zodiacally backward, and the great age started by Pisces could be seen to run from when Hipparchus was at his prime, and on to a date now still almost a century ahead for the start of the fresh Aquarius dimension of human destiny. Many astrologers and occultists accept this hypothesis, and there are other theories with current acceptance. If, for example, the foundation of the exceptionally unique United States in 1776 is to be taken as the beginning of the epochal Aquarian Age, then the launching of the Piscean epoch in ancient history would have rather rough correspondence to

Alexander the Great and leading on to the Romans and a new sort of Western world as presumably epitomizing such a marked expansion of human culture on the previous occasion.

It is far simpler to start from present times in determining the Piscean beginnings. What became the complete overturn of the long-established competitive economic system of the civilized globe with the Great Depression starting in 1929, and ultimately involving every industrialized nation very seriously, is exceptionally epochal. When this was followed by the controlled release of atomic energy as of key uniqueness in 1942, and perhaps the sending of men to the moon and bringing them back safely only twenty-seven years later in 1969, there is an extent of enduring change for all men everywhere with nothing of equally wide consequence anywhere at any accurately known moment of the past nineteen centuries at least. Here virtually today is the extraordinary distinction to be expected of any new great age in comparison with the preceding one. Exactness to a single year is of course impossible because of overlap and spread of global relationships. The thirteen years from 1929 to 1942, or even the forty years from 1929 to 1969, do not overextend the practical concept of "now".

There has been a marked astrological buttressing for this assumption, together with testimony to a remarkable build-up toward new Aquarian Age opportunities for fully two centuries now. Most exceptional has been the discovery of three additional planets, now in very general use by astrologers and of the greatest and most particular service to a truly modern astrology. It must be remembered that astrology measures man's experience primarily, and so while these outlying bodies were present in the heavens they were not visible to him and thus no part of his experienced awareness. Uranus might possibly have been seen as a planet, but it never was. In any practical horoscopic sense the three additional moving stars did not exist astrologically. Thus they fundamentally identify matters, or areas of his concern, such as could not possibly have been brought to his realization in the earlier times. Here of course is a subtle distinction that may not seem to hold at times, but can contribute to much greater incisiveness in modern analysis.

Uranus was discovered in 1781, and is identified with considerations coming into human experience with the emerging form of the unique middle-class American democracy in 1776.

Neptune was located by the astronomers in 1846, and this is in significant correspondence to the Communistic Manifesto of 1848 and the effective emergence of a strange social consciousness in which sovereignty is vested in the masses. Quite aside from the basic significance is that the developing Communism soon became a dictatorship of the proletariat, taken over by its own elite group in the exercise of quite old-fashioned exploitation.

Pluto had its discovery in 1930 in close correspondence to the Great Depression of 1929, and in consequence can be seen to be prime indicator of Aquarian Age potentials and actuality. The Piscean Age may, therefore, be well characterized by the absence of what the newly-discovered planets have come to indicate, and even more by what, in modern life, is under globe-wide elimination. Mankind's colonial development, that began to have its definite breakup with World War I in 1914 and was largely preliminary to the 1929 financial debacle is disappearing. That was the special era of politico-commercial or socioeconomic monopoly or aggrandisement brought to characteristic form by Alexander's generals after his death in 323 B.C., and expanded in due course by the Romans. The invention of coinage by the Lydians in the sixth century B.C. may have contributed significantly to the then emerging Piscean dimension which exhibited freer human intercourse, and very significantly could have been the beginnings of the individual horoscope and the great personal phase of astrology (by the Greeks around the fourth century B.C.). But speculation along this line has very sharp limitations when carried back into not-too-well documented or understood ancient days.

Of the five planets, or "movable stars" of the ancients,

Saturn and Jupiter stood apart because of the regularity of their performance in their annual retrogradation during their very slow circuit of the zodiac in nearly thirty and some twelve years respectively. This separateness from the other three planets gave these two a basic distinction, and it was a beginning of what, in modern times, would be an establishment of the very definite and astrologically effective planetary departments. Next to be taken, in a measure of special affinity with each other, were the three other true solar planets brought to more erratic behavior through their closer linkage by orbit with the sun. The two inferior bodies, as Venus and Mercury are designated by the astronomers, are carried around the zodiacal circle quite completely each year. This is the fundamental fact that gives them their horoscopic roles. Mars, conversely, is a superior planet in astronomical description, and has a less close tie with the luminary but nonetheless exhibits an irregularity of retrogradation very much akin to that of Venus. Again there is here a distinct planetary department. The other two departments thereupon become (1) the luminaries, and, in present days, (2) the three newly-discovered bodies in orbit out farther from the sun.

THE SUN, or the greater light or luminary, as the center of the solar system, represents the core of everything of immediate concern in the astronomer's perspective. In taking the place of the earth, or the physical core of all reality known by man and pertinent to him, it is representative astrologically both of his immediate world of experience and of himself in his psychological or overall totality. This matter of remaining at the center of whatever exists or happens is necessarily primary in all realization, and so in astrology it is identified, in essentially dynamic fashion, as simple and unalloyed PURPOSE. The symbol is the circle which rather frequently represents spirit or completeness, or the transcendence of physical limitation in everyday practical fulfillment, with a dot in the center to show this operating or the ability to operate in this fashion. Here is man himself at core, in terms of his absolute individuality, and therefore, at least potentially, at the center of control of virtually anything in any respect. In practical reality the indication is of simple self, and this is the signification widely used by astrologers.

There is an astronomical symbol for the earth, consisting of a circle with an inscribed cross, and in astrology this represents the part of fortune or a symbolical factor of broad use in a more detailed delineation that will not have attention in this simplified text. It may be seen however in the usual horoscope.

THE MOON, as the astrologer's lesser light or luminary, derives its signification from the fact that it is a single satellite of the earth, for which the sun in the earth-centered perspective of astrology has become completely representative. This adds up to an unvarying subservience of the secondary to the major body and, in consequence, to a general signification by the moon of the particular total of everything over and above the basic identity of man or of any pertinent entity. In balance with self, the symbolization of this closely linked factor is thus of whatever lies exterior in any respect to that self. Here, astrologically, is the fundamental indication of not-self, or particularly (1) in the largest sense the public or general affairs as there happens to be individual reaction to them and, (2) in the smaller sense the personal relevance of everyday realities usually known through FEELING. The symbolism is the moon's first crescent, which astronomically suggests the ready availability of the basic substance of human experience.

The sun and moon constitute the planetary department of vitality, or of selfhood in its simple and basic operation.

There are two additional symbols that may be seen in the usual horoscope, but that are not important enough for consideration here. They consist of an eye for a garment hook frontside up and down respectively, and indicate in order the north and south nodes of the moon.

MARS is one of the three planets of simple practicality in everyday existence. They constitute the planetary department of EFFICIENCY. Mars, as the superior or outer planet in this practical group, reveals the essentially spontaneous INITIATIVE of man's everyday activities. Here is the familiar interactivity of people in their accustomed co-operation with each other, in (1) the various phases of starting or beginning and, (2) any continuing, or effort to continue, in the overall action of self-expression. The symbol is the circle of spirit or basic all-inclusiveness, surmounted by the cross of matter usually modified as a pointed spear.

VENUS, in the department of efficiency, is what is simply the reverse sort of self-expression in comparison with Mars. As an inward-lying planet relative to the earth in orbit and so with closing-in rather than reaching-out significance, it charts a gathering to self in balance with self's projection of itself in the same practicality of everyday reality. Instead of starting, this is finishing or various phases of completion. Instead of showing action being taken or its continuance, it shows collection in the form of cherishing and enjoying and enhancing. This is a trait of attention to pertinent elements of not-self in distinction from concern over the more positive act of basic self-expression. It is the manifestation of ACQUISITIVENESS in familiar relations and so has long been seen as the indicator of (1) love or special satisfaction on the psychological side and, (2) possessions or wealth on the physical. The symbol is the circle of spirit or basic all-inclusiveness surmounting the symbolical cross of matter or material substantiation.

MERCURY, as the third member of the department of efficiency, is next to the sun itself in the solar system, and represents an explorative or tentative projection of purpose or human will or fundamental identity into the practical or everyday world in order to establish an overall harmonization of the starting and finishing activities of experience. This is a bringing of everyday experience to an ordering realization, and it becomes MENTALITY as the delineative role of this planet. Here is the essential skill of man. The symbol is a combination of the cross of matter undergirding a circle of all-inclusiveness, as with Venus, with both surmounted by a half-circle lying on its side. That uppermost part of the symbol might be recognized as an exaggerated modification of the spear of Mars, rather than as the unquestionably more obvious crescent of the moon. The latter however has general acceptance.

JUPITER in the solar system is the innermost one of the only two outlying and, so perhaps more individualistic, planets known to the ancients, as in contrast with Mars and Venus and especially Mercury. This might well have suggested a correlation of the more splendid Jupiter with traits of a sheer individual distinctiveness, or a conscious existence marked by whatever self-consistency man might possess. Here would be potential escape from the surface limitations of everyday reality, and so leading to the traditional identification of the planet as the great benefic. Thus represented is the manifestation of personality as the positive factor in a planetary department of MOTIVATION or moral and essentially private existence, and the manifestation of this by Jupiter is identified astrologically as ENTHUSIASM. The symbol is the cross of matter or material substantiation with the crescent of man's fundamental involvement in commonplace existence perched on its eastward point, and so suggesting a measure of control of his own experience or in general at least an unfettered utilization of it.

SATURN, as outermost in the planetary department of motivation, came naturally enough to represent the outer cosmos at large, or external reality as a whole in its limitation upon, or its challenge to, personal existence. Also the early astrologers presumably noted the suggestive correlation between the roughly twenty-nine years of this moveable star's cycle and the approximate twenty-nine days of the moon's zodiacal circuit, and so conceived an overall everything-else as a universal public of sorts with which it would be necessary to deal. This of course would be the notion of destiny or of consequences arising from the essential nature of an overall totality. As fate it was what in time degenerated to a guarantee of calamity. But such a cosmic ordering is in balance with self-disciplined individuality, in a universe of never ending flux of which great advantage can be taken in parallel with the very great disadvantage that may no less be suffered. There must be a proper approach to the opportunity of it all at best, and the possibility of that is stressed in the keyword SENSITIVENESS. Here in simple fact is human wisdom. The symbol shows a somewhat modified crescent of feeling suspended from the lower leg of the cross of matter or material substantiation, to suggest perhaps an introspection in living as well as effective employment of the general everything-else of life.

URANUS is the first-located and nearest inward of the three newly-discovered planets in the solar system that now have come to comprise an astrological department of SIGNIFICANCE. Its delineative suggestiveness through the correspondence of its discovery to the emergence of the unique form of American democracy has been noted, and this has suggested its designation by the keyword INDEPENDENCE. Here essentially is human dignity elevated to a vital place in modern social development. The symbol is quite arbitrary. At one time it was a modified Mars. Now it usually is a capital "H", for the astronomer Herschel who discovered it, with a planet suspended from the crossbar.

NEPTUNE, as the solar satellite with its orbit next out into the heavens, and the second planet in establishing a department of significance, has been seen in similar fashion to have a basic correspondence to the emergence of the social consciousness of modern humanity in the 1840's. The conception of a sovereignty in the masses, and developing its real genius in an increasingly middle-class dominance of the industrial society, has suggested the planet's designation as OBLIGATION. This essentially is a sophisticated or truly new age responsibility. Its symbol is the familiar trident of the sea god.

PLUTO, as the recently located and outermost planet in the solar system now expanding a department of significance, has been shown to have dramatic correspondence to the start in a total economic reconstruction of the entire globe together with the launching of the epochal nuclear dispensation of human history. Here is potentiality calling for the greatest sort of depth in dedication on the part of mankind, and this suggested the designation of Pluto as OBSESSION. This essentially is a totally enlightened advancement of man's refinement as characteristic of the incoming Aquarian Age. The two symbols in use are a modified "P" in astronomical publications, and in most current astrological materials the circle of spirit held in what has been identified as a chalice of experience.

These are the ten planets that in a personal astrology chart the characteristic traits of human activity in the context of the cosmic order that facilitates their operation.

## TABLE D
## THE PLANETARY KEYWORDS

*Vitality*

| Sun | - | Purpose | | Moon | - | Feeling |
|---|---|---|---|---|---|---|

*Efficiency*

| Mars | - | Initiative | - | Venus | - | Acquisitiveness |
|---|---|---|---|---|---|---|
| | | Mercury | - | Mentality | | |

*Motivation*

| Jupiter | - | Enthusiasm | | Saturn | - | Sensitiveness |
|---|---|---|---|---|---|---|

*Significance*

| Uranus | - | Independence | - | Neptune | - | Obligation |
|---|---|---|---|---|---|---|
| | | Pluto | - | Obsession | | |

*Not Within the Scope of These Pages*

Moon's north node                    Moon's south node

Part of Fortune

# Chapter Three
## LIFE'S PLANETARY CYCLES

In the simplest operation of a personal astrology, and of primary importance perhaps, are characteristic periods of human affairs marked off by planetary cycles in the heavens. Of these cycles the ones established in turn by those planets more and more distant from the sun, and so progressively slower and slower in moving around the zodiac, identify greater and greater length of duration for some certain phases of conscious existence. Naturally they should therefore have increasing significance for man in general. Four, at least, of these cyclic manifestations can be sketched out in a way to apply to everybody for this final quarter of the current century, without any necessity for the reader to refer to some astrological tabulation of the shifting planetary positions in the heavens. The method is to consider the transit or passage of each outlying planet through the zodiacal signs.

There are some difficulties both in charting and interpreting these cycles, but these need not be of too great concern. All the true solar planets, in the perspective from the earth on which man actually exists, have regular periods of retrogradation or backward motion in the zodiac and so may back out of a sign and then enter it again. Consequently the cycles may not have single or simple beginning and end. But it is possible to adjust to this. All people do not react in the same way to the shifts in their general environment, because every environment has striking differences precisely as these people have. Certain natural phenomena may be identical in some special manifestation over a broad area, but the individuals in that area will not all be concerned in the same manner. Thus when it rains, some have to go out and others can remain in, and any needed adjustment is usually very easy. Astrologically it merely is necessary to describe each cycle so that its pertinence can be seen in the light of all the principal traits of character and

32

make-up of each person involved, and so at best enabling him to grasp and take advantage of the given trend in the general eventuation.

At this point of exposition, in dramatizing the overall significance of the basic cycles, the irregularities due to retrogradation will be ignored. That is, for convenience, the time of ingress into each sign will be averaged. Astrology is a symbolical science, and while nicety of precision has its place it may be of no assistance whatsoever to the neophyte in cases such as here. Personal response to far-reaching shifts involving everybody can hardly ever be exact in the day and hour of individual differences.

## THE PLUTO CYCLES

PLUTO ENTERED LIBRA in 1971, and inaugurated a major cycle of some thirteen years' duration. Astrologically this is a proposition of OBSESSION in EQUIVALENCE, and thus a time of unusual effort to further the levelling out of human society in the new Aquarian dispensation. This would be through the actions and influence of dramatically, and even violently, concerned people more or less everywhere. Adjustment to the tendency would mean a widening acceptance of the more fundamentally seminal events and, at best, a contribution to their fulfillment. This phase of history had its most important evidence of itself in the United States through the development of the Watergate scandal in national politics, as events came into the open with the arrest of the five wiretappers in Washington on June 17, 1972.

PLUTO ENTERS SCORPIO in 1984 to inaugurate a major cycle of some eleven years' duration. Astrologically this is a proposition of OBSESSION in CREATIVITY, and thus a time of unusual effort to encourage science and invention and also to achieve a broadening scope of personal interrelations in establishing the new Aquarian Age of human society. Adjustment to the tendency would mean highly individual participation in developing the epochal concern over man's everyday self-fulfillment.

PLUTO ENTERS SAGITTARIUS in 1995 to inaugurate a

major cycle of some thirteen or more years' duration. Astrologically this is a proposition of OBSESSION in ADMINISTRATION, and thus a time of unusual effort to reorganize the whole global structure of human society and so compel a public interest in every possible genius of man's practical nature in the shaping of the new Aquarian Age. Adjustment to this tendency would mean every possible worthwhile and personal contribution to the new striking international developments.

## THE NEPTUNE CYCLES

NEPTUNE ENTERED SAGITTARIUS in 1970 and inaugurated a major cycle of some fourteen years' duration. Astrologically this is a proposition of OBLIGATION in ADMINISTRATION, and thus a time of special encouragement of local autonomy in each or all dimensions of human group interest. The world saw the swing to relatively small homogeneous political entities, and the increase in sociopolitical fragmentation or excessive nationalism is a manifestation of the trend. Here is significance through the dramatic actions and influence of highly public-spirited people as the happy side of it all. Adjustment to the tendency would mean widening acceptance and employment of the specific value of every individual's cultural heritage. This phase of history had its most important manifestation of itself for the United States with its real turn away, at long last, from the role it had assumed as the righteous policeman of the nations, or in the gradual withdrawal of its armed forces from Viet Nam that had began on a small scale in the early summer of 1969.

NEPTUNE ENTERS CAPRICORN in 1984 to inaugurate a major cycle of some thirteen years' duration. Astrologically this is a proposition of OBLIGATION in DISCRIMINATION, and thus a time of special encouragement of more comprehensive international law and more effective rapprochement among interrelated cultural and political groups around the globe. Adjustment to the tendency would mean a growing and worldwide tendency to social and political adroitness in the repair at all points of human group co-operation and economic interchange.

NEPTUNE ENTERS AQUARIUS in 1997 to inaugurate a major cycle of some fourteen years' duration. Astrologically this is a proposition of OBLIGATION in LOYALTY, and thus a time of special encouragement for widening and increasingly the varied affiliations needed in strengthening the socio-economic structure of the Aquarian Age. Adjustment to the tendency would mean a much more effective division of labor in personal concerns and interest in order to cultivate the well-rounded individuality of the new order.

## THE URANUS CYCLES

URANUS ENTERED SCORPIO in 1974 and inaugurated a major cycle of some seven years' duration. Astrologically this is a proposition of INDEPENDENCE in CREATIVITY, and thus a time of special need for a characteristic self-integration in order to accomplish anything of any enduring worth at this historical moment. Adjustment to the tendency would mean a perhaps continuous reordering of himself by every person seeking any real distinction. This phase of history had dramatic evidence of itself in the spring of this year with the quick demoralization and then total collapse of South Viet Nam when any hope of adequate and continuous shoring up by the United States became altogether dissipated.

URANUS ENTERS SAGITTARIUS in 1981 to inaugurate a major cycle of some seven years' duration. Astrologically this is a proposition of INDEPENDENCE in ADMINISTRATION, and thus a time of special need for the stabilization of all new-found integrations through some practical distribution of their fruits or potentialities. Adjustment to the tendency would be in definite self-alignment to the greater opportunity at all points.

URANUS ENTERS CAPRICORN in 1988 to inaugurate a major cycle of some seven years' duration. Astrologically this is a proposition of INDEPENDENCE in DISCRIMINATION, and thus a time of special need for the proving out and dramatization of the worth and enduring pertinence of everything coming to any personal concern. Adjustment to the tendency would be, at best, a new dignity of self-anchorage in the basic substance of all individual relationships.

URANUS ENTERS AQUARIUS in 1995 to inaugurate a major cycle of some seven years' duration. Astrologically this is a proposition of INDEPENDENCE in LOYALTY, and thus a time of special need for thoroughgoing self-alignment to people and causes of common concern and potentiality. Adjustment to the tendency would be, at best, a complete confidence in the ultimate validity of the endless social reordering everywhere and a ready fellowship with the phases of it that can be furthered or supported in any way.

## THE SATURN CYCLES

With the indications of the planets on the basis of their transits through the zodiacal signs greatly narrowed in scope at this point, through cycles of approximately a mere two and a half years' duration, there is a falling back to areas of human everyday realities that have been charted by astrology almost from the first development of the individual horoscope by the ancient Greeks. But if these are more immediate and, by and large, much more trivial matters to take into account, they still are of consequence for all people everywhere. These particular ingresses have always had serious attention by astrologers.

SATURN ENTERED CANCER in 1973 and inaugurated a cycle of SENSITIVENESS in EXPANSION. This would mean effective awareness as an emphasized public need for expansion in everyday affairs, or the encouraged effort to achieve it. It was dramatized by the successful counter to a military superiority of Israel through the effective cartel of the Arabs and the increase of the price of oil by 400% in the twelve months from October in 1973. Personal adjustment in this context would be to the emerging shift in economical balance around the globe in its varying individual impact.

SATURN ENTERED LEO in 1975 to inaugurate a cycle of SENSITIVENESS in ASSURANCE. This would mean a strong emphasis on leadership with exceptional attempts to bring outstanding individuals to positions of particular responsibility. Personal adjustment, at best, would consist of grasping every opportunity to capitulate on individual personal experience.

SATURN ENTERS VIRGO in 1977 to inaugurate a cycle of SENSITIVENESS in ASSIMILATION. This would mean a period of consolidation of gains, or capitalization on the general drift of events at large. Personal adjustment, at best, would be through psychological housecleaning, and the cultivating of greater efficiency in private affairs.

SATURN ENTERS LIBRA in 1980 to inaugurate a cycle of SENSITIVENESS in EQUIVALENCE. This would mean a period of radical change in the trial-and-error balance of life, with every possible reinforcement of the normal co-operations in everyday living. Personal adjustment, at best, would be a thorough updating of all human relations and general concerns of any current pertinence.

SATURN ENTERS SCORPIO in 1982 to inaugurate a cycle of SENSITIVENESS in CREATIVITY. This would mean a period of possible spectacular manifestation of man's genuine skills and certainly a continuing progress in his mastery of nature. Personal adjustment, at best, would be through meeting some challenge to genuine individual achievement in his own affairs at least.

SATURN ENTERS SAGITTARIUS in 1985 to inaugurate a cycle of SENSITIVENESS in ADMINISTRATION. This would mean a period of intensified aggregations of people, or unusually broad and significant launching of shared effort and common rehearsal of group realities. Personal adjustment, at best, would be by a thoroughgoing plunge into the loosened opportunities of both communal and global projects of the especially humanistic explosion of the moment.

SATURN ENTERS CAPRICORN in 1988 to inaugurate a cycle of SENSITIVENESS in DISCRIMINATION. This would mean a period of widespread settling down of things, and perhaps much more comprehension in economics and science and religion. Personal adjustment, at best, would be a parallel better ordering of everything of individual interest and concern.

SATURN ENTERS AQUARIUS in 1991 to inaugurate a cycle of

SENSITIVENESS in LOYALTY. This would mean a period of widespread awakening to unrealized values in everyday existence, and of possible marked development of appreciation for the elements of the new Aquarian age now increasingly manifest. Personal adjustment, at best, would be through a definite firming of belief and self-commitment in every phase of daily life.

SATURN ENTERS PISCES in 1993 to inaugurate a cycle of SENSITIVENESS in SYMPATHY. This would mean a period when people would find it unusually easy to associate with each other in much greater mutual enterprise, and thus gain larger perspectives of enduring value. Personal adjustment, at best, would be through much less inhibited activity in all areas of self-expression.

SATURN ENTERS ARIES in 1996 to inaugurate a cycle of SENSITIVENESS in ASPIRATION. This would mean a period when men and women would be exceptionally inclined to reach out from their own fruits of experience to embrace each other in many phases of common ambition and perhaps seek encouragement for very vital accomplishments of their own. Personal adjustment, at best, would be through genuine analysis of their purpose in life, and of the potentials to be developed.

SATURN ENTERS TAURUS in 1998 to inaugurate a cycle of SENSITIVENESS in VIRILITY. This would mean a period when people at large would be inclined toward every self-stimulating surge of individual energy, or appetite for experience, and so toward definite action along all lines of self-ambition. Personal adjustment, at best, would be through an increasingly open attitude in everyday living, together with a thoroughly vigorous participation in the various high tides of human developments at this point.

SATURN ENTERS GEMINI in 2000 to inaugurate a cycle of SENSITIVENESS in VIVIFICATION. This would mean a period when everybody may well be caught up in the fullness of some special potential, or marked culmination of their individual effort of some sort. Personal adjustment, at best, would be a specific endeavor to increase the dimension or significance of the basic joy of self-projection through all life.

## THE SUN CYCLES

It is possible to continue with the sun in the pattern of this Part One of the present exposition, thanks to the regularity of its movement on the one hand and the broad public familiarity with the twelvefold sunsign division of the year on the other. There still is the lack of precise beginnings and ends for each successive period, without recourse to astrological tables as will be explained later in these pages, but the necessary generalization at this stage can continue to be of great value or practical usefulness.

THE PRESENCE OF THE SUN IN ARIES IS ESSENTIALLY from March 21 to April 19, and it reveals the traditional springtime point in life, where human ASPIRATION may most likely emerge on its own and gain its most commonplace encouragement. Adjustment to this monthly trend should be, a thoroughgoing psychological dismissal of needless prejudices and no longer significant frustrations.

THE PRESENCE OF THE SUN IN TAURUS IS ESSENTIALLY from April 20 through May 20, and it reveals the annual mobilization of the energies of self when human VIRILITY gains its fresh impetus for the year. Adjustment to this monthly trend, should be a thoroughgoing inventory of the fundamental self-capacity.

THE PRESENCE OF THE SUN IN GEMINI IS ESSENTIALLY from May 21 to June 20, and it reveals the traditional VIVIFICATION, or experimental outreach, into anything or everything convenient for the quickening of self and others to practical manifestation. Adjustment to this monthly trend should be a thoroughgoing self-exercise.

THE PRESENCE OF THE SUN IN CANCER IS ESSENTIALLY from June 21 to July 22, and it reveals the traditional summertime point in life where human EXPANSION gains its greatest facilitation from all the exceptional intermingling and ramifying activities. Adjustment to this monthly trend should be some effective grasp of the fruits of experience both psychologically and in practical actuality.

THE PRESENCE OF THE SUN IN LEO IS ESSENTIALLY from July 23 to August 22, and it reveals the traditional mobilization of ASSURANCE in character as well as in ability to project the image of self in profitable directness. Adjustment to this monthly trend should be a thoroughgoing realization and validation of the enduring substance of individuality.

THE PRESENCE OF THE SUN IN VIRGO IS ESSENTIALLY from August 23 to September 22 and it reveals the traditional consummatory period in experience for vital ASSIMILATION into self of the worthwhile elements of individual existence and now apt to have unusual encouragement. Adjustment to this monthly trend should be a thoroughgoing house-cleaning in the personal economy.

THE PRESENCE OF THE SUN IN LIBRA IS ESSENTIALLY from September 23 to October 22 and it reveals the traditional autumnal point in experience where a basic individual EQUIVALENCE can help reorient life effectively in every pre-vailing complex of practical or everyday relevance. Ad-justment to this monthly trend should be a thoroughgoing acceptance of all pertinent harmony of establishment or true co-operation.

THE PRESENCE OF THE SUN IN SCORPIO IS ESSENTIALLY from October 23 to November 21 and it reveals the traditional mobilization of man's inner powers when external or more tangible opportunity begins to call out the CREATIVITY of a more transcendental effectiveness. Adjustment to this monthly trend should be a thoroughgoing capitalization on all personal development.

THE PRESENCE OF THE SUN IN SAGITTARIUS IS ESSENTIALLY from November 22 to December 21, and it reveals the traditional uninhibited projection of self into all life in an enlistment of its potentials through ADMINISTRATION for performance in fundamental and dramatic evidence of itself. Adjustment to this monthly trend should be an un-ceasing and thoroughgoing effort to bring everyday realities into definitive relevance.

THE PRESENCE OF THE SUN IN CAPRICORN IS ESSENTIALLY from December 22 to January 19 and it reveals the tradi-tional wintertime point in life where human DISCRIM-INATION is brought to the most critical and enduring dem-onstration of itself. Adjustment to this monthly trend should be an uncompromisingly impartial judgment on anything and everything coming to any personal concern.

THE PRESENCE OF THE SUN IN AQUARIUS IS ESSENTIALLY from January 20 to February 18 and it reveals the traditional period in experience when man is most called upon to recognize and to hold all phases of LOYALTY in his experience. Adjustment to this monthly trend should be a thorough re-established self-anchorage in the enduring values he has been able to make his own.

THE PRESENCE OF THE SUN IN PISCES IS ESSENTIALLY from February 19 to March 20 and it reveals the traditional and highly sentimental point in life where a genuine SYMPATHY is demanded of mankind, or where the insights and ascetic value of others may be shared in a culminating breadth of human relationship. Adjustment to this monthly trend should be a thoroughgoing rounding out of individual consciousness in some deeply challenging dimension.

## THE MOON CYCLES

In the case of the lesser luminary there is the regularity of zodiacal performance characterizing the sun, or greater luminary. Also there is wide public acquaintance with certain of its features that can have practical employment at this point, but the moon's transits of the zodiacal signs must have their consideration in Part Two of this text. Attention must now be given to its phases, which are commonly known and found on calendars or in almanacs. In clear weather they can actually be seen and watched in the skies.

An almost universal procedure is to distinguish between the times when the moon is increasing in light, as the older books describe it, or contrariwise is decreasing. Wholly apart from astrology, there is a very considerable host of farmers on down through natural-food devotees and amateur gardners who plant by the moon. The astrological dictum for almost all professionals or students is to avoid starting anything of real importance after the lunar orb has reached its full and then progressively loses its illumination, or until the next new moon.

This of course can become nonsensical, rational oversimplification. Obviously, the world would about fall to pieces if nobody really began anything through half the time of his life. What will be helpful, rather, is a distinction whereby consideration (1) is a matter of capitalizing on what is in progress in contrast with (2) recognizing the state of affairs where the capitalization may be consummated. This is a proposition of operating within the pattern of the lunar gravitation, and for the individual it is largely a psychological self-ordering. The physical gravitation of the moon is literally potent enough in the phenomenon of the ocean tides, among the many things of common observation, and quite possibly, according to current scientific theory, even in the utterly remote and slow procession of the equinoxes.

## THE PLANETARY HOURS

Here is another phase of the simple personal astrology in which the living with the stars requires no astrological calculation or horoscopic reference on the part of anyone making use of the book.

The basis of these short little periods, not necessarily of an even sixty minutes of the clock, is a planetary rulership that the ancients gave to each hour of the day as well as to each day and week. The fundamental arrangement of the days in their sequence (Monday, Tuesday, etc.) has been a matter of familiar acceptance from almost the dawn of man's recorded history. That this is essentially astrological in nature is revealed by the planetary order that characterizes it.

Thus the planets are taken in order of their orbits from Saturn as outermost in the then-known solar system, through the sun in the earth's orbit, and on down to Mercury and finally the terrestrial satellite — the moon — as the seventh factor. It is not unlikely that the symbolizing intellect of antiquity took the curious parallel in the cycles of Saturn and the moon, or the roughly twenty-nine years and twenty-nine days respectively, as revealing a chain of heavenly relationship brought around into a circle. In ef-

fect a new Saturn would always follow each terminal moon
in endless succession. This is illustrated in the diagram by
the lines following the relationship of days and hours in
astrological distribution of the heavenly system of orbit.

## DAY AND HOUR RULERSHIPS

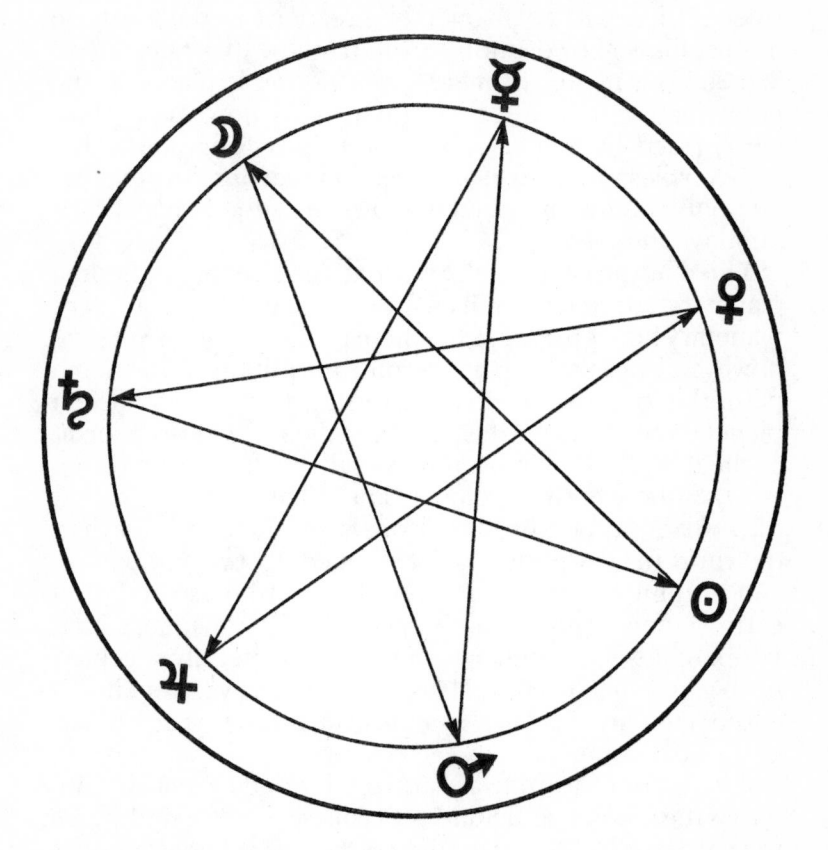

The division of a day into twelve-hour halves results from
the earth's rotation of its axis, in rough parallel to the
establishment of the twelve months in a measure of its
annual revolution. The probable evolution of the idea, that

brought the sevenfold and twelvefold factors to a determination of planetary rulerships for the hours and days of human existence, was possibly the endless sequence of the original seven significators through a series of seven, twenty-four-hour days. This would be twelve from sunrise to sunset, and twelve from sunset to sunrise. When this is done, the planet turning up first for each day becomes the ruler of that particular one. The reader can demonstrate this for himself by counting around on the diagram. There Saturn, as a matter of mere convenience, is placed at the point that would be the ascendant of a horoscope. This hour, ruled by Saturn, starts the twenty-four hours that Saturn rules, or Saturday. Three times around or twenty-one plus three more planets shows the sun as the start of Sunday, and so on.

This diagram starts with Saturday because the traditional planetary sequence begins with that planet. The tables of planetary hours presented in these pages start with Sunday, however, since that also has become a tradition. To be noted parenthetically is a rather interesting fact in this ancient planetary sequence — the placing of the sun where the orbit of the earth lies is almost unimpeachable indication of the fact that these early astrologers knew that the sun circuited the zodiac only because it took on the motion of the earth in the third orbital position. It exhibited no retrogradation, and nothing suggested any possibility of an astronomical earth-centered universe. Indeed, there is evidence that Hipparchus was familiar with the now generally accepted heliocentric perspective. He rejected it however, and influenced Ptolemy, because to him in his day it seemed unnecessarily complex.

Apart from Saturday as Saturn's day and certainly Monday as the moon's, and Sunday of course, there is nothing in the names of the others to suggest their astrological nature. Tuesday's designation comes from the Old English Tiw, or a god of war, to suggest the ruling Mars. Wednesday got its name from Wodan or an Anglo-Saxon deity associated with the Scandinavian Odin who, among other characteristics, was a god of wisdom and thus representative of Mercury at least in part. Thursday is named from the Scandinavian Thor, or very much a twin of sorts of the Greek Zeus or Roman Jupiter. Friday was given a feminine designation out of the early North European mythology, and taken to represent Frigg, who was the wife of Odin and a goddess of marital bliss.

In general, the rulership of the day is much less vital than that of the hour since it is an unchanging constant for that twenty-four hours, and every individual has made a more or less permanent adjustment to this in his general make-up. Frequently an individual learns that his Wednesdays, so to speak, have a regularity of character to which he is long accustomed. This of course can be quite subjective, and in most cases of little importance.

The planetary hours now presented have been newly calculated by computer, and they are tabulated in local mean time. They are not the regularized or precise sixty-minute intervals ticked off by a clock but rather a twelfth of the time span from sunrise to sunset and then continuing as twelfths from sunset to sunrise. For using them it may be necessary to have access to an atlas, to find the geographical latitude at the place where they are to be used. Interpolation or proportional adjustment may, of course, be necessary for a desired preciseness. Thus for terrestrial latitude of 46° it will be necessary to take one fifth of the difference in time shown for a given hour in the tables for 45° and 50° in order to correct 45° for 46° and so on. These few minutes will seldom amount to much, and the correction hardly needs to be made when there is no effort to use a planetary hour at the very threshold of its effectiveness. Much more important are the basic and generally preliminary clock-time corrections. Daylight-saving must be corrected to standard time before all else, and it may be necessary to make a careful check to find in what standard time zone an individual is functioning since this is frequently a most erratic proposition of wholly local determination. Standard time of course is an hour earlier than daylight saving. If the latter is 4:00 p.m. the former is 3:00 p.m., and that is what must be employed.

It may be necessary again to refer to an atlas to find the terrestrial longitude of the place where these astrological hours are to be used. If this is somewhere west of the terrestrial longitude of 90° west that mark off central standard time, correction is necessary on the basis of four minutes by the clock for each longitudinal degree of difference. Hence if the planetary hours are to be determined at Omaha, Nebraska, or at approximately 96° west longitude, the difference of six degrees means 24 minutes of adjustment to make. What often makes these corrections easier to keep straight in mind is to remember that where the sun gets first, the time is later. In this example the sun has six degrees more to go westward from the central time meridian and so the mean local time is less than standard by the 24 minutes. If the mean local time taken from the tables as starting the astrological hour desired for the terrestrial latitude of Omaha is shown as 9:36 a.m. the time by the clock is 10:00 a.m. normally, or 11:00 a.m. when daylight-saving time is in effect.

## THE PLANETARY HOURS

*(The charts on these following pages are for your handy reference in finding the planetary rulers of the hours. They are presented in 24 semi-monthly charts showing the hours of the day, the days of the week and the degree of Latitude at which any individual might be residing. The reader must remember to make suitable adjustments for any variation in local times, such as Daylight Saving Time, since these charts are given in Local Mean Time.*
*—The Editor)*

## DAY HOURS: SUNRISE TO SUNSET (LOCAL MEAN TIME)

| SUN. | MON. | TU. | WED. | TH. | FRI. | SAT. | LAT. 25° | LAT. 30° | LAT. 35° | LAT. 40° | LAT. 45° | LAT. 50° | LAT. 55° | LAT. 60° |
|---|---|---|---|---|---|---|---|---|---|---|---|---|---|---|
| SUN. | MOON | MARS | MER. | JUP. | VEN. | SAT. | 6:33 | 6:38 | 6:43 | 6:49 | 6:56 | 7: 4 | 7:14 | 7:27 |
| VEN. | SAT. | SUN | MOON | MARS | MER. | JUP. | 7:30 | 7:34 | 7:38 | 7:43 | 7:49 | 7:56 | 8: 4 | 8:15 |
| MER. | JUP. | VEN. | SAT. | SUN | MOON | MARS | 8:27 | 8:30 | 8:34 | 8:38 | 8:42 | 8:48 | 8:55 | 9: 3 |
| MOON | MARS | MER. | JUP. | VEN. | SAT. | SUN. | 9:24 | 9:27 | 9:29 | 9:32 | 9:36 | 9:40 | 9:45 | 9:52 |
| SAT. | SUN | MOON | MARS | MER. | JUP. | VEN. | 10:22 | 10:23 | 10:25 | 10:27 | 10:29 | 10:32 | 10:35 | 10:40 |
| JUP. | VEN. | SAT. | SUN | MOON | MARS | MER. | 11:19 | 11:19 | 11:20 | 11:21 | 11:23 | 11:24 | 11:26 | 11:28 |
| MARS | MER. | JUP. | VEN. | SAT. | SUN | MOON | 12:16 | 12:16 | 12:16 | 12:16 | 12:16 | 12:16 | 12:16 | 12:16 |
| SUN | MOON | MARS | MER. | JUP. | VEN. | SAT. | 1:13 | 1:12 | 1:11 | 1:10 | 1: 9 | 1: 8 | 1: 6 | 1: 4 |
| VEN. | SAT. | SUN | MOON | MARS | MER. | JUP. | 2:10 | 2: 8 | 2: 7 | 2: 5 | 2: 3 | 2: 0 | 1:57 | 1:53 |
| MER. | JUP. | VEN. | SAT. | SUN | MOON | MARS | 3: 7 | 3: 5 | 3: 2 | 2:59 | 2:56 | 2:52 | 2:47 | 2:41 |
| MOON | MARS | MER. | JUP. | VEN. | SAT. | SUN | 4: 4 | 4: 1 | 3:58 | 3:54 | 3:50 | 3:44 | 3:38 | 3:29 |
| SAT. | SUN | MOON | MARS | MER. | JUP. | VEN. | 5: 1 | 4:57 | 4:53 | 4:48 | 4:43 | 4:36 | 4:28 | 4:17 |

## NIGHT HOURS: SUNSET TO SUNRISE (LOCAL MEAN TIME)

| SUN. | MON. | TU. | WED. | TH. | FRI. | SAT. | LAT. 25° | LAT. 30° | LAT. 35° | LAT. 40° | LAT. 45° | LAT. 50° | LAT. 55° | LAT. 60° |
|---|---|---|---|---|---|---|---|---|---|---|---|---|---|---|
| JUP. | VEN. | SAT. | SUN | MOON | MARS | MER. | 5:58 | 5:54 | 5:49 | 5:43 | 5:36 | 5:28 | 5:18 | 5: 5 |
| MARS | MER. | JUP. | VEN. | SAT. | SUN | MOON | 7: 1 | 6:57 | 6:53 | 6:48 | 6:43 | 6:36 | 6:28 | 6:17 |
| SUN | MOON | MARS | MER. | JUP. | VEN. | SAT. | 8: 4 | 8: 1 | 7:58 | 7:54 | 7:50 | 7:44 | 7:38 | 7:29 |
| VEN. | SAT. | SUN | MOON | MARS | MER. | JUP. | 9: 7 | 9: 5 | 9: 2 | 8:59 | 8:56 | 8:52 | 8:47 | 8:41 |
| MER. | JUP. | VEN. | SAT. | SUN | MOON | MARS | 10:10 | 10: 8 | 10: 7 | 10: 5 | 10: 3 | 10: 0 | 9:57 | 9:53 |
| MOON | MARS | MER. | JUP. | VEN. | SAT. | SUN | 11:13 | 11:12 | 11:11 | 11:10 | 11: 9 | 11: 8 | 11: 6 | 11: 4 |
| SAT. | SUN | MOON | MARS | MER. | JUP. | VEN. | 12:16 | 12:16 | 12:16 | 12:16 | 12:16 | 12:16 | 12:16 | 12:16 |
| JUP. | VEN. | SAT. | SUN | MOON | MARS | MER. | 1:19 | 1:19 | 1:20 | 1:21 | 1:23 | 1:24 | 1:26 | 1:28 |
| MARS | MER. | JUP. | VEN. | SAT. | SUN | MOON | 2:22 | 2:23 | 2:25 | 2:27 | 2:29 | 2:32 | 2:35 | 2:40 |
| SUN | MOON | MARS | MER. | JUP. | VEN. | SAT. | 3:24 | 3:27 | 3:29 | 3:32 | 3:36 | 3:40 | 3:45 | 3:52 |
| VEN. | SAT. | SUN | MOON | MARS | MER. | JUP. | 4:27 | 4:30 | 4:34 | 4:38 | 4:42 | 4:48 | 4:55 | 5: 3 |
| MER. | JUP. | VEN. | SAT. | SUN | MOON | MARS | 5:30 | 5:34 | 5:38 | 5:43 | 5:49 | 5:56 | 6: 4 | 6:15 |

## DAY HOURS: SUNRISE TO SUNSET (LOCAL MEAN TIME)

| SUN. | MON. | TU. | WED. | TH. | FRI. | SAT. | LAT. 25° | LAT. 30° | LAT. 35° | LAT. 40° | LAT. 45° | LAT. 50° | LAT. 55° | LAT. 60° |
|---|---|---|---|---|---|---|---|---|---|---|---|---|---|---|
| SUN | MOON | MARS | MER. | JUP. | VEN. | SAT. | 6:43 | 6:50 | 6:58 | 7: 7 | 7:17 | 7:29 | 7:45 | 8: 5 |
| VEN. | SAT. | SUN | MOON | MARS | MER. | JUP. | 7:39 | 7:44 | 7:51 | 7:58 | 8: 7 | 8:17 | 8:30 | 8:47 |
| MER. | JUP. | VEN. | SAT. | SUN | MOON | MARS | 8:34 | 8:39 | 8:44 | 8:50 | 8:57 | 9: 5 | 9:15 | 9:29 |
| MOON | MARS | MER. | JUP. | VEN. | SAT. | SUN | 9:30 | 9:33 | 9:37 | 9:42 | 9:47 | 9:53 | 10: 1 | 10:11 |
| SAT. | SUN | MOON | MARS | MER. | JUP. | VEN. | 10:25 | 10:28 | 10:30 | 10:33 | 10:37 | 10:41 | 10:46 | 10:53 |
| JUP. | VEN. | SAT. | SUN | MOON | MARS | MER. | 11:21 | 11:22 | 11:23 | 11:25 | 11:27 | 11:29 | 11:31 | 11:35 |
| MARS | MER. | JUP. | VEN. | SAT. | SUN | MOON | 12:16 | 12:16 | 12:16 | 12:16 | 12:17 | 12:17 | 12:17 | 12:17 |
| SUN | MOON | MARS | MER. | JUP. | VEN. | SAT. | 1:12 | 1:11 | 1:10 | 1: 8 | 1: 6 | 1: 4 | 1: 2 | 12:59 |
| VEN. | SAT. | SUN | MOON | MARS | MER. | JUP. | 2: 7 | 2: 5 | 2: 3 | 2: 0 | 1:56 | 1:52 | 1:47 | 1:40 |
| MER. | JUP. | VEN. | SAT. | SUN | MOON | MARS | 3: 3 | 3: 0 | 2:56 | 2:51 | 2:46 | 2:40 | 2:33 | 2:22 |
| MOON | MARS | MER. | JUP. | VEN. | SAT. | SUN | 3:59 | 3:54 | 3:49 | 3:43 | 3:36 | 3:28 | 3:18 | 3: 4 |
| SAT. | SUN | MOON | MARS | MER. | JUP. | VEN. | 4:54 | 4:48 | 4:42 | 4:35 | 4:26 | 4:16 | 4: 3 | 3:46 |

## NIGHT HOURS: SUNSET TO SUNRISE (LOCAL MEAN TIME)

| SUN. | MON. | TU. | WED. | TH. | FRI. | SAT. | LAT. 25° | LAT. 30° | LAT. 35° | LAT. 40° | LAT. 45° | LAT. 50° | LAT. 55° | LAT. 60° |
|---|---|---|---|---|---|---|---|---|---|---|---|---|---|---|
| JUP. | VEN. | SAT. | SUN | MOON | MARS | MER. | 5:50 | 5:43 | 5:35 | 5:26 | 5:16 | 5: 4 | 4:49 | 4:28 |
| MARS | MER. | JUP. | VEN. | SAT. | SUN | MOON | 6:54 | 6:48 | 6:42 | 6:35 | 6:26 | 6:16 | 6: 3 | 5:46 |
| SUN | MOON | MARS | MER. | JUP. | VEN. | SAT. | 7:59 | 7:54 | 7:49 | 7:43 | 7:36 | 7:28 | 7:18 | 7: 4 |
| VEN. | SAT. | SUN | MOON | MARS | MER. | JUP. | 9: 3 | 9: 0 | 8:56 | 8:51 | 8:46 | 8:40 | 8:33 | 8:22 |
| MER. | JUP. | VEN. | SAT. | SUN | MOON | MARS | 10: 7 | 10: 5 | 10: 3 | 10: 0 | 9:56 | 9:52 | 9:47 | 9:40 |
| MOON | MARS | MER. | JUP. | VEN. | SAT. | SUN | 11:12 | 11:11 | 11:10 | 11: 8 | 11: 6 | 11: 4 | 11: 2 | 10:59 |
| SAT. | SUN | MOON | MARS | MER. | JUP. | VEN. | 12:16 | 12:16 | 12:16 | 12:16 | 12:17 | 12:17 | 12:17 | 12:17 |
| JUP. | VEN. | SAT. | SUN | MOON | MARS | MER. | 1:21 | 1:22 | 1:23 | 1:25 | 1:27 | 1:29 | 1:31 | 1:35 |
| MARS | MER. | JUP. | VEN. | SAT. | SUN | MOON | 2:25 | 2:28 | 2:30 | 2:33 | 2:37 | 2:41 | 2:46 | 2:53 |
| SUN | MOON | MARS | MER. | JUP. | VEN. | SAT. | 3:30 | 3:33 | 3:37 | 3:42 | 3:47 | 3:53 | 4: 1 | 4:11 |
| VEN. | SAT. | SUN | MOON | MARS | MER. | JUP. | 4:34 | 4:39 | 4:44 | 4:50 | 4:57 | 5: 5 | 5:15 | 5:29 |
| MER. | JUP. | VEN. | SAT. | SUN | MOON | MARS | 5:39 | 5:44 | 5:51 | 5:58 | 6: 7 | 6:17 | 6:30 | 6:47 |

# JANUARY 16 TO 31, ANY YEAR

## DAY HOURS: SUNRISE TO SUNSET (LOCAL MEAN TIME)

| SUN. | MON. | TU. | WED. | TH. | FRI. | SAT. | LAT. 25° | LAT. 30° | LAT. 35° | LAT. 40° | LAT. 45° | LAT. 50° | LAT. 55° | LAT. 60° |
|---|---|---|---|---|---|---|---|---|---|---|---|---|---|---|
| SUN | MOON | MARS | MER. | JUP. | VEN. | SAT. | 6:50 | 6:59 | 7: 9 | 7:20 | 7:34 | 7:51 | 8:12 | 8:41 |
| VEN. | SAT. | SUN | MOON | MARS | MER. | JUP. | 7:44 | 7:51 | 8: 0 | 8: 9 | 8:21 | 8:35 | 8:52 | 9:16 |
| MER. | JUP. | VEN. | SAT. | SUN | MOON | MARS | 8:38 | 8:44 | 8:51 | 8:58 | 9: 7 | 9:18 | 9:33 | 9:52 |
| MOON | MARS | MER. | JUP. | VEN. | SAT. | SUN. | 9:32 | 9:36 | 9:42 | 9:47 | 9:54 | 10: 2 | 10:13 | 10:27 |
| SAT. | SUN | MOON | MARS | MER. | JUP. | VEN. | 10:26 | 10:29 | 10:32 | 10:36 | 10:41 | 10:46 | 10:54 | 11: 2 |
| JUP. | VEN. | SAT. | SUN | MOON | MARS | MER. | 11:20 | 11:22 | 11:23 | 11:25 | 11:28 | 11:30 | 11:34 | 11:37 |
| MARS | MER. | JUP. | VEN. | SAT. | SUN | MOON | 12:14 | 12:14 | 12:14 | 12:14 | 12:14 | 12:14 | 12:14 | 12:12 |
| SUN | MOON | MARS | MER. | JUP. | VEN. | SAT. | 1: 8 | 1: 7 | 1: 5 | 1: 3 | 1: 1 | 12:58 | 12:55 | 12:48 |
| VEN. | SAT. | SUN | MOON | MARS | MER. | JUP. | 2: 2 | 1:59 | 1:56 | 1:52 | 1:48 | 1:42 | 1:35 | 1:23 |
| MER. | JUP. | VEN. | SAT. | SUN | MOON | MARS | 2:57 | 2:52 | 2:47 | 2:41 | 2:35 | 2:26 | 2:16 | 1:58 |
| MOON | MARS | MER. | JUP. | VEN. | SAT. | SUN | 3:51 | 3:45 | 3:38 | 3:30 | 3:21 | 3:10 | 2:56 | 2:33 |
| SAT. | SUN | MOON | MARS | MER. | JUP. | VEN. | 4:45 | 4:37 | 4:29 | 4:19 | 4: 8 | 3:54 | 3:37 | 3: 9 |

## NIGHT HOURS: SUNSET TO SUNRISE (LOCAL MEAN TIME)

| SUN. | MON. | TU. | WED. | TH. | FRI. | SAT. | LAT. 25° | LAT. 30° | LAT. 35° | LAT. 40° | LAT. 45° | LAT. 50° | LAT. 55° | LAT. 60° |
|---|---|---|---|---|---|---|---|---|---|---|---|---|---|---|
| JUP. | VEN. | SAT. | SUN | MOON | MARS | MER. | 5:39 | 5:30 | 5:20 | 5: 8 | 4:55 | 4:38 | 4:17 | 3:44 |
| MARS | MER. | JUP. | VEN. | SAT. | SUN | MOON | 6:45 | 6:37 | 6:29 | 6:19 | 6: 8 | 5:54 | 5:37 | 5: 9 |
| SUN | MOON | MARS | MER. | JUP. | VEN. | SAT. | 7:51 | 7:45 | 7:38 | 7:30 | 7:21 | 7:10 | 6:56 | 6:33 |
| VEN. | SAT. | SUN | MOON | MARS | MER. | JUP. | 8:57 | 8:52 | 8:47 | 8:41 | 8:35 | 8:26 | 8:16 | 7:58 |
| MER. | JUP. | VEN. | SAT. | SUN | MOON | MARS | 10: 2 | 9:59 | 9:56 | 9:52 | 9:48 | 9:42 | 9:35 | 9:23 |
| MOON | MARS | MER. | JUP. | VEN. | SAT. | SUN | 11: 8 | 11: 7 | 11: 5 | 11: 3 | 11: 1 | 10:58 | 10:55 | 10:48 |
| SAT. | SUN | MOON | MARS | MER. | JUP. | VEN. | 12:14 | 12:14 | 12:14 | 12:14 | 12:14 | 12:14 | 12:14 | 12:12 |
| JUP. | VEN. | SAT. | SUN | MOON | MARS | MER. | 1:20 | 1:22 | 1:23 | 1:25 | 1:28 | 1:30 | 1:34 | 1:37 |
| MARS | MER. | JUP. | VEN. | SAT. | SUN | MOON | 2:26 | 2:29 | 2:32 | 2:36 | 2:41 | 2:46 | 2:54 | 3: 2 |
| SUN | MOON | MARS | MER. | JUP. | VEN. | SAT. | 3:32 | 3:36 | 3:42 | 3:47 | 3:54 | 4: 2 | 4:13 | 4:27 |
| VEN. | SAT. | SUN | MOON | MARS | MER. | JUP. | 4:38 | 4:44 | 4:51 | 4:58 | 5: 7 | 5:18 | 5:33 | 5:52 |
| MER. | JUP. | VEN. | SAT. | SUN | MOON | MARS | 5:44 | 5:51 | 6: 0 | 6: 9 | 6:21 | 6:35 | 6:52 | 7:16 |

# JANUARY 1 TO 15, ANY YEAR

## DAY HOURS: SUNRISE TO SUNSET (LOCAL MEAN TIME)

| SUN. | MON. | TU. | WED. | TH. | FRI. | SAT. | LAT. 25° | LAT. 30° | LAT. 35° | LAT. 40° | LAT. 45° | LAT. 50° | LAT. 55° | LAT. 60° |
|---|---|---|---|---|---|---|---|---|---|---|---|---|---|---|
| SUN | MOON | MARS | MER. | JUP. | VEN. | SAT. | 6:51 | 7: 1 | 7:13 | 7:27 | 7:43 | 8: 4 | 8:30 | 9: 7 |
| VEN. | SAT. | SUN | MOON | MARS | MER. | JUP. | 7:44 | 7:53 | 8: 3 | 8:14 | 8:27 | 8:44 | 9: 6 | 9:37 |
| MER. | JUP. | VEN. | SAT. | SUN | MOON | MARS | 8:37 | 8:44 | 8:52 | 9: 0 | 9:11 | 9:25 | 9:42 | 10: 7 |
| MOON | MARS | MER. | JUP. | VEN. | SAT. | SUN. | 9:30 | 9:35 | 9:41 | 9:47 | 9:55 | 10: 5 | 10:18 | 10:37 |
| SAT. | SUN | MOON | MARS | MER. | JUP. | VEN. | 10:23 | 10:26 | 10:30 | 10:34 | 10:39 | 10:46 | 10:55 | 11: 7 |
| JUP. | VEN. | SAT. | SUN | MOON | MARS | MER. | 11:16 | 11:18 | 11:20 | 11:20 | 11:23 | 11:26 | 11:31 | 11:37 |
| MARS | MER. | JUP. | VEN. | SAT. | SUN | MOON | 12: 9 | 12: 9 | 12: 9 | 12: 7 | 12: 7 | 12: 7 | 12: 7 | 12: 7 |
| SUN | MOON | MARS | MER. | JUP. | VEN. | SAT. | 1: 2 | 1: 0 | 12:58 | 12:53 | 12:51 | 12:47 | 12:43 | 12:37 |
| VEN. | SAT. | SUN | MOON | MARS | MER. | JUP. | 1:55 | 1:51 | 1:47 | 1:40 | 1:35 | 1:28 | 1:19 | 1: 7 |
| MER. | JUP. | VEN. | SAT. | SUN | MOON | MARS | 2:48 | 2:42 | 2:36 | 2:27 | 2:19 | 2: 9 | 1:55 | 1:37 |
| MOON | MARS | MER. | JUP. | VEN. | SAT. | SUN | 3:41 | 3:34 | 3:26 | 3:13 | 3: 2 | 2:49 | 2:32 | 2: 7 |
| SAT. | SUN | MOON | MARS | MER. | JUP. | VEN. | 4:34 | 4:25 | 4:15 | 4: 0 | 3:46 | 3:30 | 3: 8 | 2:36 |

## NIGHT HOURS: SUNSET TO SUNRISE (LOCAL MEAN TIME)

| SUN. | MON. | TU. | WED. | TH. | FRI. | SAT. | LAT. 25° | LAT. 30° | LAT. 35° | LAT. 40° | LAT. 45° | LAT. 50° | LAT. 55° | LAT. 60° |
|---|---|---|---|---|---|---|---|---|---|---|---|---|---|---|
| JUP. | VEN. | SAT. | SUN | MOON | MARS | MER. | 5:27 | 5:16 | 5: 4 | 4:47 | 4:30 | 4:10 | 3:44 | 3: 6 |
| MARS | MER. | JUP. | VEN. | SAT. | SUN | MOON | 6:34 | 6:25 | 6:15 | 6: 0 | 5:46 | 5:30 | 5: 8 | 4:36 |
| SUN | MOON | MARS | MER. | JUP. | VEN. | SAT. | 7:41 | 7:34 | 7:26 | 7:13 | 7: 2 | 6:49 | 6:32 | 6: 7 |
| VEN. | SAT. | SUN | MOON | MARS | MER. | JUP. | 8:48 | 8:42 | 8:36 | 8:27 | 8:19 | 8: 9 | 7:55 | 7:37 |
| MER. | JUP. | VEN. | SAT. | SUN | MOON | MARS | 9:55 | 9:51 | 9:47 | 9:40 | 9:35 | 9:28 | 9:19 | 9: 7 |
| MOON | MARS | MER. | JUP. | VEN. | SAT. | SUN | 11: 2 | 11: 0 | 10:58 | 10:53 | 10:51 | 10:47 | 10:43 | 10:37 |
| SAT. | SUN | MOON | MARS | MER. | JUP. | VEN. | 12: 9 | 12: 9 | 12: 9 | 12: 7 | 12: 7 | 12: 7 | 12: 7 | 12: 7 |
| JUP. | VEN. | SAT. | SUN | MOON | MARS | MER. | 1:16 | 1:18 | 1:20 | 1:20 | 1:23 | 1:26 | 1:31 | 1:37 |
| MARS | MER. | JUP. | VEN. | SAT. | SUN | MOON | 2:23 | 2:26 | 2:30 | 2:34 | 2:39 | 2:46 | 2:55 | 3: 7 |
| SUN | MOON | MARS | MER. | JUP. | VEN. | SAT. | 3:30 | 3:35 | 3:41 | 3:47 | 3:55 | 4: 5 | 4:18 | 4:37 |
| VEN. | SAT. | SUN | MOON | MARS | MER. | JUP. | 4:37 | 4:44 | 4:52 | 5: 0 | 5:11 | 5:25 | 5:42 | 6: 7 |
| MER. | JUP. | VEN. | SAT. | SUN | MOON | MARS | 5:44 | 5:53 | 6: 3 | 6:14 | 6:27 | 6:44 | 7: 6 | 7:37 |

# MARCH 1 TO 15, ANY YEAR

## DAY HOURS: SUNRISE TO SUNSET (LOCAL MEAN TIME)

| SUN. | MON. | TU. | WED. | TH. | FRI. | SAT. | LAT. 25° | LAT. 30° | LAT. 35° | LAT. 40° | LAT. 45° | LAT. 50° | LAT. 55° | LAT. 60° |
|------|------|-----|------|-----|------|------|------|------|------|------|------|------|------|------|
| SUN | MOON | MARS | MER. | JUP. | VEN. | SAT. | 6:20 | 6:23 | 6:25 | 6:28 | 6:31 | 6:35 | 6:40 | 6:46 |
| VEN. | SAT. | SUN | MOON | MARS | MER. | JUP. | 7:19 | 7:21 | 7:23 | 7:25 | 7:28 | 7:31 | 7:35 | 7:41 |
| MER. | JUP. | VEN. | SAT. | SUN. | MOON | MARS | 8:18 | 8:19 | 8:21 | 8:23 | 8:25 | 8:28 | 8:31 | 8:35 |
| MOON | MARS | MER. | JUP. | VEN. | SAT. | SUN. | 9:17 | 9:18 | 9:19 | 9:21 | 9:22 | 9:24 | 9:27 | 9:30 |
| SAT. | SUN | MOON | MARS | MER. | JUP. | VEN. | 10:16 | 10:16 | 10:17 | 10:18 | 10:19 | 10:21 | 10:22 | 10:24 |
| JUP. | VEN. | SAT. | SUN | MOON | MARS | MER. | 11:14 | 11:15 | 11:16 | 11:16 | 11:16 | 11:17 | 11:18 | 11:19 |
| MARS | MER. | JUP. | VEN. | SAT. | SUN | MOON | 12:13 | 12:13 | 12:13 | 12:13 | 12:13 | 12:13 | 12:13 | 12:14 |
| SUN | MOON | MARS | MER. | JUP. | VEN. | SAT. | 1:12 | 1:12 | 1:11 | 1:11 | 1:10 | 1:10 | 1:9 | 1:8 |
| VEN. | SAT. | SUN | MOON | MARS | MER. | JUP. | 2:11 | 2:10 | 2:9 | 2:8 | 2:7 | 2:6 | 2:5 | 2:3 |
| MER. | JUP. | VEN. | SAT. | SUN | MOON | MARS | 3:9 | 3:8 | 3:7 | 3:6 | 3:4 | 3:3 | 3:0 | 2:57 |
| MOON | MARS | MER. | JUP. | VEN. | SAT. | SUN | 4:8 | 4:7 | 4:5 | 4:3 | 4:1 | 3:59 | 3:56 | 3:52 |
| SAT. | SUN | MOON | MARS | MER. | JUP. | VEN. | 5:7 | 5:5 | 5:3 | 5:1 | 4:58 | 4:55 | 4:51 | 4:47 |

## NIGHT HOURS: SUNSET TO SUNRISE (LOCAL MEAN TIME)

| SUN. | MON. | TU. | WED. | TH. | FRI. | SAT. | LAT. 25° | LAT. 30° | LAT. 35° | LAT. 40° | LAT. 45° | LAT. 50° | LAT. 55° | LAT. 60° |
|------|------|-----|------|-----|------|------|------|------|------|------|------|------|------|------|
| JUP. | VEN. | SAT. | SUN | MOON | MARS | MER. | 6:6 | 6:4 | 6:1 | 5:59 | 5:55 | 5:52 | 5:47 | 5:41 |
| MARS | MER. | JUP. | VEN. | SAT. | SUN | MOON | 7:7 | 7:5 | 7:3 | 7:1 | 6:58 | 6:55 | 6:51 | 6:47 |
| SUN | MOON | MARS | MER. | JUP. | VEN. | SAT. | 8:8 | 8:7 | 8:5 | 8:3 | 8:1 | 7:59 | 7:56 | 7:52 |
| VEN. | SAT. | SUN | MOON | MARS | MER. | JUP. | 9:9 | 9:8 | 9:7 | 9:6 | 9:4 | 9:3 | 9:0 | 8:57 |
| MER. | JUP. | VEN. | SAT. | SUN | MOON | MARS | 10:11 | 10:10 | 10:9 | 10:8 | 10:7 | 10:6 | 10:5 | 10:3 |
| MOON | MARS | MER. | JUP. | VEN. | SAT. | SUN | 11:12 | 11:12 | 11:11 | 11:11 | 11:10 | 11:10 | 11:9 | 11:8 |
| SAT. | SUN | MOON | MARS | MER. | JUP. | VEN. | 12:13 | 12:13 | 12:13 | 12:13 | 12:13 | 12:13 | 12:13 | 12:14 |
| JUP. | VEN. | SAT. | SUN | MOON | MARS | MER. | 1:14 | 1:15 | 1:15 | 1:16 | 1:16 | 1:17 | 1:18 | 1:19 |
| MARS | MER. | JUP. | VEN. | SAT. | SUN | MOON | 2:16 | 2:16 | 2:17 | 2:18 | 2:19 | 2:21 | 2:22 | 2:24 |
| SUN | MOON | MARS | MER. | JUP. | VEN. | SAT. | 3:17 | 3:18 | 3:19 | 3:21 | 3:22 | 3:24 | 3:27 | 3:30 |
| VEN. | SAT. | SUN | MOON | MARS | MER. | JUP. | 4:18 | 4:19 | 4:21 | 4:23 | 4:25 | 4:28 | 4:31 | 4:35 |
| MER. | JUP. | VEN. | SAT. | SUN | MOON | MARS | 5:19 | 5:21 | 5:23 | 5:25 | 5:28 | 5:31 | 5:35 | 5:41 |

# MARCH 16 TO 31, ANY YEAR

## DAY HOURS: SUNRISE TO SUNSET (LOCAL MEAN TIME)

| SUN. | MON. | TU. | WED. | TH. | FRI. | SAT. | LAT. 25° | LAT. 30° | LAT. 35° | LAT. 40° | LAT. 45° | LAT. 50° | LAT. 55° | LAT. 60° |
|---|---|---|---|---|---|---|---|---|---|---|---|---|---|---|
| SUN | MOON | MARS | MER. | JUP. | VEN. | SAT. | 6: 4 | 6: 4 | 6: 3 | 6: 2 | 6: 1 | 6: 0 | 5:59 | 5:58 |
| VEN. | SAT. | SUN | MOON | MARS | MER. | JUP. | 7: 5 | 7: 5 | 7: 4 | 7: 3 | 7: 3 | 7: 2 | 7: 1 | 7: 0 |
| MER. | JUP. | VEN. | SAT. | SUN | MOON | MARS | 8: 6 | 8: 5 | 8: 5 | 8: 4 | 8: 4 | 8: 3 | 8: 2 | 8: 1 |
| MOON | MARS | MER. | JUP. | VEN. | SAT. | SUN | 9: 6 | 9: 6 | 9: 6 | 9: 5 | 9: 5 | 9: 5 | 9: 4 | 9: 3 |
| SAT. | SUN | MOON | MARS | MER. | JUP. | VEN. | 10: 7 | 10: 7 | 10: 7 | 10: 7 | 10: 6 | 10: 6 | 10: 6 | 10: 5 |
| JUP. | VEN. | SAT. | SUN | MOON | MARS | MER. | 11: 8 | 11: 8 | 11: 8 | 11: 8 | 11: 8 | 11: 7 | 11: 7 | 11: 7 |
| MARS | MER. | JUP. | VEN. | SAT. | SUN | MOON | 12: 9 | 12: 9 | 12: 9 | 12: 9 | 12: 9 | 12: 9 | 12: 9 | 12: 9 |
| SUN | MOON | MARS | MER. | JUP. | VEN. | SAT. | 1: 9 | 1: 9 | 1:10 | 1:10 | 1:10 | 1:10 | 1:11 | 1:11 |
| VEN. | SAT. | SUN | MOON | MARS | MER. | JUP. | 2:10 | 2:10 | 2:11 | 2:11 | 2:11 | 2:12 | 2:12 | 2:13 |
| MER. | JUP. | VEN. | SAT. | SUN | MOON | MARS | 3:11 | 3:11 | 3:12 | 3:12 | 3:13 | 3:13 | 3:14 | 3:15 |
| MOON | MARS | MER. | JUP. | VEN. | SAT. | SUN | 4:12 | 4:12 | 4:13 | 4:13 | 4:14 | 4:15 | 4:16 | 4:17 |
| SAT. | SUN | MOON | MARS | MER. | JUP. | VEN. | 5:12 | 5:13 | 5:13 | 5:14 | 5:15 | 5:16 | 5:17 | 5:19 |

## NIGHT HOURS: SUNSET TO SUNRISE (LOCAL MEAN TIME)

| SUN. | MON. | TU. | WED. | TH. | FRI. | SAT. | LAT. 25° | LAT. 30° | LAT. 35° | LAT. 40° | LAT. 45° | LAT. 50° | LAT. 55° | LAT. 60° |
|---|---|---|---|---|---|---|---|---|---|---|---|---|---|---|
| JUP. | VEN. | SAT. | SUN | MOON | MARS | MER. | 6:13 | 6:14 | 6:14 | 6:15 | 6:16 | 6:17 | 6:19 | 6:21 |
| MARS | MER. | JUP. | VEN. | SAT. | SUN | MOON | 7:12 | 7:13 | 7:13 | 7:14 | 7:15 | 7:16 | 7:17 | 7:19 |
| SUN | MOON | MARS | MER. | JUP. | VEN. | SAT. | 8:12 | 8:12 | 8:13 | 8:13 | 8:14 | 8:15 | 8:16 | 8:17 |
| VEN. | SAT. | SUN | MOON | MARS | MER. | JUP. | 9:11 | 9:11 | 9:12 | 9:12 | 9:13 | 9:13 | 9:14 | 9:15 |
| MER. | JUP. | VEN. | SAT. | SUN | MOON | MARS | 10:10 | 10:10 | 10:11 | 10:11 | 10:11 | 10:12 | 10:12 | 10:13 |
| MOON | MARS | MER. | JUP. | VEN. | SAT. | SUN | 11: 9 | 11: 9 | 11:10 | 11:10 | 11:10 | 11:10 | 11:11 | 11:11 |
| SAT. | SUN | MOON | MARS | MER. | JUP. | VEN. | 12: 9 | 12: 9 | 12: 9 | 12: 9 | 12: 9 | 12: 9 | 12: 9 | 12: 9 |
| JUP. | VEN. | SAT. | SUN | MOON | MARS | MER. | 1: 8 | 1: 8 | 1: 8 | 1: 8 | 1: 8 | 1: 7 | 1: 7 | 1: 7 |
| MARS | MER. | JUP. | VEN. | SAT. | SUN | MOON | 2: 7 | 2: 7 | 2: 7 | 2: 6 | 2: 6 | 2: 6 | 2: 6 | 2: 5 |
| SUN | MOON | MARS | MER. | JUP. | VEN. | SAT. | 3: 6 | 3: 6 | 3: 6 | 3: 5 | 3: 5 | 3: 5 | 3: 5 | 3: 3 |
| VEN. | SAT. | SUN | MOON | MARS | MER. | JUP. | 4: 6 | 4: 5 | 4: 5 | 4: 4 | 4: 4 | 4: 3 | 4: 2 | 4: 1 |
| MER. | JUP. | VEN. | SAT. | SUN | MOON | MARS | 5: 5 | 5: 4 | 5: 4 | 5: 3 | 5: 3 | 5: 2 | 5: 1 | 5: 0 |

## DAY HOURS: SUNRISE TO SUNSET (LOCAL MEAN TIME)

| SUN. | MON. | TU. | WED. | TH. | FRI. | SAT. | LAT. 25° | LAT. 30° | LAT. 35° | LAT. 40° | LAT. 45° | LAT. 50° | LAT. 55° | LAT. 60° |
|---|---|---|---|---|---|---|---|---|---|---|---|---|---|---|
| SUN | MOON | MARS | MER. | JUP. | VEN. | SAT. | 5:49 | 5:46 | 5:42 | 5:38 | 5:34 | 5:28 | 5:21 | 5:13 |
| VEN. | SAT. | SUN | MOON | MARS | MER. | JUP. | 6:51 | 6:49 | 6:46 | 6:43 | 6:39 | 6:34 | 6:29 | 6:21 |
| MER. | JUP. | VEN. | SAT. | SUN | MOON | MARS | 7:54 | 7:52 | 7:50 | 7:47 | 7:44 | 7:40 | 7:36 | 7:30 |
| MOON | MARS | MER. | JUP. | VEN. | SAT. | SUN | 8:56 | 8:55 | 8:53 | 8:51 | 8:49 | 8:46 | 8:43 | 8:39 |
| SAT. | SUN | MOON | MARS | MER. | JUP. | VEN. | 9:59 | 9:58 | 9:57 | 9:56 | 9:54 | 9:52 | 9:50 | 9:47 |
| JUP. | VEN. | SAT. | SUN | MOON | MARS | MER. | 11: 2 | 11: 1 | 11: 1 | 11: 0 | 10:59 | 10:58 | 10:57 | 10:56 |
| MARS | MER. | JUP. | VEN. | SAT. | SUN | MOON | 12: 4 | 12: 4 | 12: 4 | 12: 4 | 12: 4 | 12: 4 | 12: 5 | 12: 5 |
| SUN | MOON | MARS | MER. | JUP. | VEN. | SAT. | 1: 7 | 1: 7 | 1: 8 | 1: 9 | 1:10 | 1:11 | 1:12 | 1:13 |
| VEN. | SAT. | SUN | MOON | MARS | MER. | JUP. | 2: 9 | 2:10 | 2:12 | 2:13 | 2:15 | 2:17 | 2:19 | 2:22 |
| MER. | JUP. | VEN. | SAT. | SUN | MOON | MARS | 3:12 | 3:13 | 3:15 | 3:17 | 3:20 | 3:23 | 3:26 | 3:31 |
| MOON | MARS | MER. | JUP. | VEN. | SAT. | SUN | 4:14 | 4:17 | 4:19 | 4:22 | 4:25 | 4:29 | 4:33 | 4:40 |
| SAT. | SUN | MOON | MARS | MER. | JUP. | VEN. | 5:17 | 5:20 | 5:23 | 5:26 | 5:30 | 5:35 | 5:41 | 5:48 |

## NIGHT HOURS: SUNSET TO SUNRISE (LOCAL MEAN TIME)

| SUN. | MON. | TU. | WED. | TH. | FRI. | SAT. | LAT. 25° | LAT. 30° | LAT. 35° | LAT. 40° | LAT. 45° | LAT. 50° | LAT. 55° | LAT. 60° |
|---|---|---|---|---|---|---|---|---|---|---|---|---|---|---|
| JUP. | VEN. | SAT. | SUN | MOON | MARS | MER. | 6:19 | 6:23 | 6:26 | 6:30 | 6:35 | 6:41 | 6:48 | 6:57 |
| MARS | MER. | JUP. | VEN. | SAT. | SUN | MOON | 7:17 | 7:20 | 7:23 | 7:26 | 7:30 | 7:35 | 7:41 | 7:48 |
| SUN | MOON | MARS | MER. | JUP. | VEN. | SAT. | 8:14 | 8:17 | 8:19 | 8:22 | 8:25 | 8:29 | 8:33 | 8:40 |
| VEN. | SAT. | SUN | MOON | MARS | MER. | JUP. | 9:12 | 9:13 | 9:15 | 9:17 | 9:20 | 9:23 | 9:26 | 9:31 |
| MER. | JUP. | VEN. | SAT. | SUN | MOON | MARS | 10: 9 | 10:10 | 10:12 | 10:13 | 10:15 | 10:17 | 10:19 | 10:22 |
| MOON | MARS | MER. | JUP. | VEN. | SAT. | SUN | 11: 7 | 11: 7 | 11: 8 | 11: 9 | 11:10 | 11:11 | 11:12 | 11:13 |
| SAT. | SUN | MOON | MARS | MER. | JUP. | VEN. | 12: 4 | 12: 4 | 12: 4 | 12: 4 | 12: 4 | 12: 4 | 12: 5 | 12: 5 |
| JUP. | VEN. | SAT. | SUN | MOON | MARS | MER. | 1: 2 | 1: 1 | 1: 1 | 1: 0 | 12:59 | 12:58 | 12:57 | 12:56 |
| MARS | MER. | JUP. | VEN. | SAT. | SUN | MOON | 1:59 | 1:58 | 1:57 | 1:56 | 1:54 | 1:52 | 1:50 | 1:47 |
| SUN | MOON | MARS | MER. | JUP. | VEN. | SAT. | 2:56 | 2:55 | 2:53 | 2:51 | 2:49 | 2:46 | 2:43 | 2:39 |
| VEN. | SAT. | SUN | MOON | MARS | MER. | JUP. | 3:54 | 3:52 | 3:50 | 3:47 | 3:44 | 3:40 | 3:36 | 3:30 |
| MER. | JUP. | VEN. | SAT. | SUN | MOON | MARS | 4:51 | 4:49 | 4:46 | 4:43 | 4:39 | 4:34 | 4:29 | 4:21 |

# APRIL 16 TO 30, ANY YEAR

## DAY HOURS: SUNRISE TO SUNSET (LOCAL MEAN TIME)

| SUN. | MON. | TU. | WED. | TH. | FRI. | SAT. | LAT. 25° | LAT. 30° | LAT. 35° | LAT. 40° | LAT. 45° | LAT. 50° | LAT. 55° | LAT. 60° |
|---|---|---|---|---|---|---|---|---|---|---|---|---|---|---|
| SUN | MOON | MARS | MER. | JUP. | VEN. | SAT. | 5:35 | 5:29 | 5:23 | 5:16 | 5: 8 | 4:58 | 4:45 | 4:29 |
| VEN. | SAT. | SUN | MOON | MARS | MER. | JUP. | 6:39 | 6:34 | 6:29 | 6:23 | 6:16 | 6: 8 | 5:58 | 5:44 |
| MER. | JUP. | VEN. | SAT. | SUN | MOON | MARS | 7:43 | 7:40 | 7:36 | 7:31 | 7:25 | 7:19 | 7:11 | 7: 0 |
| MOON | MARS | MER. | JUP. | VEN. | SAT. | SUN | 8:48 | 8:45 | 8:42 | 8:38 | 8:34 | 8:29 | 8:23 | 8:15 |
| SAT. | SUN | MOON | MARS | MER. | JUP. | VEN. | 9:52 | 9:50 | 9:48 | 9:46 | 9:43 | 9:40 | 9:36 | 9:30 |
| JUP. | VEN. | SAT. | SUN | MOON | MARS | MER. | 10:56 | 10:55 | 10:54 | 10:53 | 10:52 | 10:50 | 10:48 | 10:46 |
| MARS | MER. | JUP. | VEN. | SAT. | SUN | MOON | 12: 1 | 12: 1 | 12: 1 | 12: 1 | 12: 1 | 12: 1 | 12: 1 | 12: 1 |
| SUN | MOON | MARS | MER. | JUP. | VEN. | SAT. | 1: 5 | 1: 6 | 1: 7 | 1: 8 | 1:10 | 1:11 | 1:14 | 1:17 |
| VEN. | SAT. | SUN | MOON | MARS | MER. | JUP. | 2: 9 | 2:11 | 2:13 | 2:16 | 2:18 | 2:22 | 2:25 | 2:32 |
| MER. | JUP. | VEN. | SAT. | SUN | MOON | MARS | 3:13 | 3:16 | 3:19 | 3:23 | 3:27 | 3:32 | 3:39 | 3:47 |
| MOON | MARS | MER. | JUP. | VEN. | SAT. | SUN | 4:18 | 4:21 | 4:26 | 4:31 | 4:36 | 4:43 | 4:51 | 5: 3 |
| SAT. | SUN | MOON | MARS | MER. | JUP. | VEN. | 5:22 | 5:27 | 5:32 | 5:38 | 5:45 | 5:54 | 6: 4 | 6:18 |

## NIGHT HOURS: SUNSET TO SUNRISE (LOCAL MEAN TIME)

| SUN. | MON. | TU. | WED. | TH. | FRI. | SAT. | LAT. 25° | LAT. 30° | LAT. 35° | LAT. 40° | LAT. 45° | LAT. 50° | LAT. 55° | LAT. 60° |
|---|---|---|---|---|---|---|---|---|---|---|---|---|---|---|
| JUP. | VEN. | SAT. | SUN | MOON | MARS | MER. | 6:26 | 6:32 | 6:38 | 6:45 | 6:54 | 7: 4 | 7:17 | 7:33 |
| MARS | MER. | JUP. | VEN. | SAT. | SUN | MOON | 7:22 | 7:27 | 7:32 | 7:38 | 7:45 | 7:54 | 8: 4 | 8:18 |
| SUN | MOON | MARS | MER. | JUP. | VEN. | SAT. | 8:18 | 8:21 | 8:26 | 8:31 | 8:36 | 8:43 | 8:51 | 9: 3 |
| VEN. | SAT. | SUN | MOON | MARS | MER. | JUP. | 9:13 | 9:16 | 9:19 | 9:23 | 9:27 | 9:32 | 9:39 | 9:47 |
| MER. | JUP. | VEN. | SAT. | SUN | MOON | MARS | 10: 9 | 10:11 | 10:13 | 10:16 | 10:18 | 10:22 | 10:26 | 10:32 |
| MOON | MARS | MER. | JUP. | VEN. | SAT. | SUN | 11: 5 | 11: 6 | 11: 6 | 11: 8 | 11:10 | 11:11 | 11:14 | 11:17 |
| SAT. | SUN | MOON | MARS | MER. | JUP. | VEN. | 12: 1 | 12: 1 | 12: 1 | 12: 1 | 12: 1 | 12: 1 | 12: 1 | 12: 1 |
| JUP. | VEN. | SAT. | SUN | MOON | MARS | MER. | 12:56 | 12:55 | 12:54 | 12:53 | 12:52 | 12:50 | 12:48 | 12:46 |
| MARS | MER. | JUP. | VEN. | SAT. | SUN | MOON | 1:52 | 1:50 | 1:48 | 1:46 | 1:43 | 1:40 | 1:36 | 1:30 |
| SUN | MOON | MARS | MER. | JUP. | VEN. | SAT. | 2:48 | 2:45 | 2:42 | 2:38 | 2:34 | 2:29 | 2:23 | 2:15 |
| VEN. | SAT. | SUN | MOON | MARS | MER. | JUP. | 3:43 | 3:40 | 3:36 | 3:31 | 3:25 | 3:19 | 3:11 | 3: 0 |
| MER. | JUP. | VEN. | SAT. | SUN | MOON | MARS | 4:39 | 4:34 | 4:29 | 4:23 | 4:16 | 4: 8 | 3:58 | 3:44 |

# MAY 1 TO 15, ANY YEAR

## DAY HOURS: SUNRISE TO SUNSET (LOCAL MEAN TIME)

| SUN. | MON. | TU. | WED. | TH. | FRI. | SAT. | LAT. 25° | LAT. 30° | LAT. 35° | LAT. 40° | LAT. 45° | LAT. 50° | LAT. 55° | LAT. 60° |
|---|---|---|---|---|---|---|---|---|---|---|---|---|---|---|
| SUN | MOON | MARS | MER. | JUP. | VEN. | SAT. | 5:24 | 5:16 | 5: 7 | 4:57 | 4:45 | 4:31 | 4:13 | 3:49 |
| VEN. | SAT. | SUN | MOON | MARS | MER. | JUP. | 6:30 | 6:23 | 6:16 | 6: 7 | 5:58 | 5:46 | 5:31 | 5:11 |
| MER. | JUP. | VEN. | SAT. | SUN | MOON | MARS | 7:35 | 7:30 | 7:24 | 7:18 | 7:10 | 7: 0 | 6:48 | 6:32 |
| MOON | MARS | MER. | JUP. | VEN. | SAT. | SUN | 8:41 | 8:37 | 8:33 | 8:28 | 8:22 | 8:15 | 8: 6 | 7:54 |
| SAT. | SUN | MOON | MARS | MER. | JUP. | VEN. | 9:47 | 9:44 | 9:42 | 9:38 | 9:34 | 9:30 | 9:24 | 9:16 |
| JUP. | VEN. | SAT. | SUN | MOON | MARS | MER. | 10:53 | 10:52 | 10:50 | 10:48 | 10:47 | 10:44 | 10:41 | 10:38 |
| MARS | MER. | JUP. | VEN. | SAT. | SUN | MOON | 11:59 | 11:59 | 11:59 | 11:59 | 11:59 | 11:59 | 11:59 | 11:59 |
| SUN | MOON | MARS | MER. | JUP. | VEN. | SAT. | 1: 4 | 1: 6 | 1: 7 | 1: 9 | 1:11 | 1:14 | 1:17 | 1:21 |
| VEN. | SAT. | SUN | MOON | MARS | MER. | JUP. | 2:10 | 2:13 | 2:16 | 2:19 | 2:23 | 2:28 | 2:34 | 2:43 |
| MER. | JUP. | VEN. | SAT. | SUN | MOON | MARS | 3:16 | 3:20 | 3:24 | 3:30 | 3:36 | 3:43 | 3:52 | 4: 4 |
| MOON | MARS | MER. | JUP. | VEN. | SAT. | SUN | 4:22 | 4:27 | 4:33 | 4:40 | 4:48 | 4:57 | 5:10 | 5:26 |
| SAT. | SUN | MOON | MARS | MER. | JUP. | VEN. | 5:28 | 5:34 | 5:42 | 5:50 | 6: 0 | 6:12 | 6:27 | 6:48 |

## NIGHT HOURS: SUNSET TO SUNRISE (LOCAL MEAN TIME)

| SUN. | MON. | TU. | WED. | TH. | FRI. | SAT. | LAT. 25° | LAT. 30° | LAT. 35° | LAT. 40° | LAT. 45° | LAT. 50° | LAT. 55° | LAT. 60° |
|---|---|---|---|---|---|---|---|---|---|---|---|---|---|---|
| JUP. | VEN. | SAT. | SUN | MOON | MARS | MER. | 6:33 | 6:41 | 6:50 | 7: 0 | 7:12 | 7:27 | 7:45 | 8:10 |
| MARS | MER. | JUP. | VEN. | SAT. | SUN | MOON | 7:28 | 7:34 | 7:42 | 7:50 | 8: 0 | 8:12 | 8:27 | 8:48 |
| SUN | MOON | MARS | MER. | JUP. | VEN. | SAT. | 8:22 | 8:27 | 8:33 | 8:40 | 8:48 | 8:57 | 9:10 | 9:26 |
| VEN. | SAT. | SUN | MOON | MARS | MER. | JUP. | 9:16 | 9:20 | 9:24 | 9:30 | 9:36 | 9:43 | 9:52 | 10: 4 |
| MER. | JUP. | VEN. | SAT. | SUN | MOON | MARS | 10:10 | 10:13 | 10:16 | 10:19 | 10:23 | 10:28 | 10:34 | 10:43 |
| MOON | MARS | MER. | JUP. | VEN. | SAT. | SUN | 11: 4 | 11: 6 | 11: 7 | 11: 9 | 11:11 | 11:14 | 11:17 | 11:21 |
| SAT. | SUN | MOON | MARS | MER. | JUP. | VEN. | 11:59 | 11:59 | 11:59 | 11:59 | 11:59 | 11:59 | 11:59 | 11:59 |
| JUP. | VEN. | SAT. | SUN | MOON | MARS | MER. | 12:53 | 12:52 | 12:50 | 12:48 | 12:47 | 12:44 | 12:41 | 12:38 |
| MARS | MER. | JUP. | VEN. | SAT. | SUN | MOON | 1:47 | 1:44 | 1:42 | 1:38 | 1:34 | 1:30 | 1:24 | 1:16 |
| SUN | MOON | MARS | MER. | JUP. | VEN. | SAT. | 2:41 | 2:37 | 2:33 | 2:28 | 2:22 | 2:15 | 2: 6 | 1:54 |
| VEN. | SAT. | SUN | MOON | MARS | MER. | JUP. | 3:35 | 3:30 | 3:24 | 3:18 | 3:10 | 3: 0 | 2:48 | 2:32 |
| MER. | JUP. | VEN. | SAT. | SUN | MOON | MARS | 4:30 | 4:23 | 4:16 | 4: 7 | 3:58 | 3:46 | 3:31 | 3:11 |

# MAY 16 TO 31, ANY YEAR

## DAY HOURS: SUNRISE TO SUNSET (LOCAL MEAN TIME)

| SUN. | MON. | TU. | WED. | TH. | FRI. | SAT. | LAT. 25° | LAT. 30° | LAT. 35° | LAT. 40° | LAT. 45° | LAT. 50° | LAT. 55° | LAT. 60° |
|---|---|---|---|---|---|---|---|---|---|---|---|---|---|---|
| SUN | MOON | MARS | MER. | JUP. | VEN. | SAT. | 5:16 | 5: 7 | 4:56 | 4:44 | 4:29 | 4:11 | 3:48 | 3:15 |
| VEN. | SAT. | SUN | MOON | MARS | MER. | JUP. | 6:24 | 6:15 | 6: 6 | 5:56 | 5:44 | 5:29 | 5:10 | 4:43 |
| MER. | JUP. | VEN. | SAT. | SUN | MOON | MARS | 7:31 | 7:24 | 7:17 | 7: 9 | 6:59 | 6:47 | 6:31 | 6:10 |
| MOON | MARS | MER. | JUP. | VEN. | SAT. | SUN | 8:38 | 8:33 | 8:27 | 8:21 | 8:14 | 8: 5 | 7:53 | 7:37 |
| SAT. | SUN | MOON | MARS | MER. | JUP. | VEN. | 9:45 | 9:41 | 9:38 | 9:34 | 9:29 | 9:23 | 9:15 | 9: 5 |
| JUP. | VEN. | SAT. | SUN | MOON | MARS | MER. | 10:52 | 10:50 | 10:48 | 10:46 | 10:44 | 10:41 | 10:37 | 10:32 |
| MARS | MER. | JUP. | VEN. | SAT. | SUN | MOON | 11:59 | 11:59 | 11:59 | 11:59 | 11:59 | 11:59 | 11:59 | 11:59 |
| SUN | MOON | MARS | MER. | JUP. | VEN. | SAT. | 1: 6 | 1: 7 | 1: 9 | 1:11 | 1:14 | 1:17 | 1:21 | 1:27 |
| VEN. | SAT. | SUN | MOON | MARS | MER. | JUP. | 2:13 | 2:16 | 2:20 | 2:24 | 2:29 | 2:35 | 2:43 | 2:54 |
| MER. | JUP. | VEN. | SAT. | SUN | MOON | MARS | 3:20 | 3:25 | 3:30 | 3:37 | 3:44 | 3:53 | 4: 5 | 4:21 |
| MOON | MARS | MER. | JUP. | VEN. | SAT. | SUN | 4:27 | 4:33 | 4:41 | 4:49 | 4:59 | 5:11 | 5:27 | 5:49 |
| SAT. | SUN | MOON | MARS | MER. | JUP. | VEN. | 5:34 | 5:42 | 5:51 | 6: 2 | 6:14 | 6:29 | 6:49 | 7:16 |

## NIGHT HOURS: SUNSET TO SUNRISE (LOCAL MEAN TIME)

| SUN. | MON. | TU. | WED. | TH. | FRI. | SAT. | LAT. 25° | LAT. 30° | LAT. 35° | LAT. 40° | LAT. 45° | LAT. 50° | LAT. 55° | LAT. 60° |
|---|---|---|---|---|---|---|---|---|---|---|---|---|---|---|
| JUP. | VEN. | SAT. | SUN | MOON | MARS | MER. | 6:41 | 6:51 | 7: 2 | 7:14 | 7:29 | 7:47 | 8:11 | 8:43 |
| MARS | MER. | JUP. | VEN. | SAT. | SUN | MOON | 7:34 | 7:42 | 7:51 | 8: 2 | 8:14 | 8:29 | 8:49 | 9:16 |
| SUN | MOON | MARS | MER. | JUP. | VEN. | SAT. | 8:27 | 8:33 | 8:41 | 8:49 | 8:59 | 9:11 | 9:27 | 9:49 |
| VEN. | SAT. | SUN | MOON | MARS | MER. | JUP. | 9:20 | 9:25 | 9:30 | 9:37 | 9:44 | 9:53 | 10: 5 | 10:21 |
| MER. | JUP. | VEN. | SAT. | SUN | MOON | MARS | 10:13 | 10:16 | 10:20 | 10:24 | 10:29 | 10:35 | 10:43 | 10:54 |
| MOON | MARS | MER. | JUP. | VEN. | SAT. | SUN | 11: 6 | 11: 7 | 11: 9 | 11:11 | 11:14 | 11:17 | 11:21 | 11:27 |
| SAT. | SUN | MOON | MARS | MER. | JUP. | VEN. | 11:59 | 11:59 | 11:59 | 11:59 | 11:59 | 11:59 | 11:59 | 11:59 |
| JUP. | VEN. | SAT. | SUN | MOON | MARS | MER. | 12:52 | 12:50 | 12:48 | 12:46 | 12:44 | 12:41 | 12:37 | 12:32 |
| MARS | MER. | JUP. | VEN. | SAT. | SUN | MOON | 1:45 | 1:41 | 1:38 | 1:34 | 1:29 | 1:23 | 1:15 | 1: 5 |
| SUN | MOON | MARS | MER. | JUP. | VEN. | SAT. | 2:38 | 2:33 | 2:27 | 2:21 | 2:14 | 2: 5 | 1:53 | 1:37 |
| VEN. | SAT. | SUN | MOON | MARS | MER. | JUP. | 3:31 | 3:24 | 3:17 | 3: 9 | 2:59 | 2:47 | 2:31 | 2:10 |
| MER. | JUP. | VEN. | SAT. | SUN | MOON | MARS | 4:24 | 4:15 | 4: 6 | 3:56 | 3:44 | 3:29 | 3:10 | 2:43 |

# JUNE 1 TO 15, ANY YEAR

## DAY HOURS: SUNRISE TO SUNSET (LOCAL MEAN TIME)

| SUN. | MON. | TU. | WED. | TH. | FRI. | SAT. | LAT. 25° | LAT. 30° | LAT. 35° | LAT. 40° | LAT. 45° | LAT. 50° | LAT. 55° | LAT. 60° |
|---|---|---|---|---|---|---|---|---|---|---|---|---|---|---|
| SUN | MOON | MARS | MER. | JUP. | VEN. | SAT. | 5:14 | 5: 3 | 4:50 | 4:36 | 4:19 | 3:59 | 3:31 | 2:52 |
| VEN. | SAT. | SUN | MOON | MARS | MER. | JUP. | 6:22 | 6:12 | 6: 2 | 5:50 | 5:36 | 5:19 | 4:56 | 4:23 |
| MER. | JUP. | VEN. | SAT. | SUN | MOON | MARS | 7:29 | 7:22 | 7:14 | 7: 4 | 6:53 | 6:39 | 6:21 | 5:55 |
| MOON | MARS | MER. | JUP. | VEN. | SAT. | SUN | 8:37 | 8:32 | 8:26 | 8:19 | 8:10 | 8: 0 | 7:46 | 7:27 |
| SAT. | SUN | MOON | MARS | MER. | JUP. | VEN. | 9:45 | 9:42 | 9:37 | 9:33 | 9:27 | 9:20 | 9:11 | 8:58 |
| JUP. | VEN. | SAT. | SUN | MOON | MARS | MER. | 10:53 | 10:51 | 10:49 | 10:47 | 10:44 | 10:41 | 10:36 | 10:30 |
| MARS | MER. | JUP. | VEN. | SAT. | SUN | MOON | 12: 1 | 12: 1 | 12: 1 | 12: 1 | 12: 1 | 12: 1 | 12: 1 | 12: 1 |
| SUN | MOON | MARS | MER. | JUP. | VEN. | SAT. | 1: 9 | 1:11 | 1:13 | 1:15 | 1:18 | 1:22 | 1:26 | 1:33 |
| VEN. | SAT. | SUN | MOON | MARS | MER. | JUP. | 2:17 | 2:20 | 2:25 | 2:29 | 2:35 | 2:42 | 2:51 | 3: 4 |
| MER. | JUP. | VEN. | SAT. | SUN | MOON | MARS | 3:25 | 3:30 | 3:36 | 3:43 | 3:52 | 4: 2 | 4:16 | 4:36 |
| MOON | MARS | MER. | JUP. | VEN. | SAT. | SUN | 4:33 | 4:40 | 4:48 | 4:58 | 5: 9 | 5:23 | 5:41 | 6: 8 |
| SAT. | SUN | MOON | MARS | MER. | JUP. | VEN. | 5:40 | 5:50 | 6: 0 | 6:12 | 6:26 | 6:43 | 7: 6 | 7:39 |

## NIGHT HOURS: SUNSET TO SUNRISE (LOCAL MEAN TIME)

| SUN. | MON. | TU. | WED. | TH. | FRI. | SAT. | LAT. 25° | LAT. 30° | LAT. 35° | LAT. 40° | LAT. 45° | LAT. 50° | LAT. 55° | LAT. 60° |
|---|---|---|---|---|---|---|---|---|---|---|---|---|---|---|
| JUP. | VEN. | SAT. | SUN | MOON | MARS | MER. | 6:48 | 6:59 | 7:12 | 7:26 | 7:43 | 8: 4 | 8:31 | 9:11 |
| MARS | MER. | JUP. | VEN. | SAT. | SUN | MOON | 7:40 | 7:50 | 8: 0 | 8:12 | 8:26 | 8:43 | 9: 6 | 9:39 |
| SUN | MOON | MARS | MER. | JUP. | VEN. | SAT. | 8:33 | 8:40 | 8:48 | 8:58 | 9: 9 | 9:23 | 9:41 | 10: 8 |
| VEN. | SAT. | SUN | MOON | MARS | MER. | JUP. | 9:25 | 9:30 | 9:36 | 9:43 | 9:52 | 10: 2 | 10:16 | 10:36 |
| MER. | JUP. | VEN. | SAT. | SUN | MOON | MARS | 10:17 | 10:20 | 10:25 | 10:29 | 10:35 | 10:42 | 10:51 | 11: 4 |
| MOON | MARS | MER. | JUP. | VEN. | SAT. | SUN | 11: 9 | 11:11 | 11:13 | 11:15 | 11:18 | 11:22 | 11:26 | 11:33 |
| SAT. | SUN | MOON | MARS | MER. | JUP. | VEN. | 12: 1 | 12: 1 | 12: 1 | 12: 1 | 12: 1 | 12: 1 | 12: 1 | 12: 1 |
| JUP. | VEN. | SAT. | SUN | MOON | MARS | MER. | 12:53 | 12:51 | 12:49 | 12:47 | 12:44 | 12:41 | 12:36 | 12:30 |
| MARS | MER. | JUP. | VEN. | SAT. | SUN | MOON | 1:45 | 1:42 | 1:37 | 1:33 | 1:27 | 1:20 | 1:11 | 12:58 |
| SUN | MOON | MARS | MER. | JUP. | VEN. | SAT. | 2:37 | 2:32 | 2:26 | 2:19 | 2:10 | 2: 0 | 1:46 | 1:27 |
| VEN. | SAT. | SUN | MOON | MARS | MER. | JUP. | 3:29 | 3:22 | 3:14 | 3: 4 | 2:53 | 2:39 | 2:21 | 1:55 |
| MER. | JUP. | VEN. | SAT. | SUN | MOON | MARS | 4:22 | 4:12 | 4: 2 | 3:50 | 3:36 | 3:19 | 2:56 | 2:23 |

## JUNE 16 TO 30, ANY YEAR

### DAY HOURS: SUNRISE TO SUNSET (LOCAL MEAN TIME)

| SUN. | MON. | TU. | WED. | TH. | FRI. | SAT. | LAT. 25° | LAT. 30° | LAT. 35° | LAT. 40° | LAT. 45° | LAT. 50° | LAT. 55° | LAT. 60° |
|---|---|---|---|---|---|---|---|---|---|---|---|---|---|---|
| SUN | MOON | MARS | MER. | JUP. | VEN. | SAT. | 5:15 | 5: 4 | 4:51 | 4:37 | 4:19 | 3:58 | 3:29 | 2:47 |
| VEN. | SAT. | SUN | MOON | MARS | MER. | JUP. | 6:23 | 6:14 | 6: 3 | 5:51 | 5:37 | 5:19 | 4:55 | 4:20 |
| MER. | JUP. | VEN. | SAT. | SUN | MOON | MARS | 7:32 | 7:24 | 7:16 | 7: 6 | 6:54 | 6:40 | 6:21 | 5:53 |
| MOON | MARS | MER. | JUP. | VEN. | SAT. | SUN | 8:40 | 8:34 | 8:28 | 8:20 | 8:12 | 8: 1 | 7:47 | 7:26 |
| SAT. | SUN | MOON | MARS | MER. | JUP. | VEN. | 9:48 | 9:44 | 9:40 | 9:35 | 9:29 | 9:22 | 9:12 | 8:58 |
| JUP. | VEN. | SAT. | SUN | MOON | MARS | MER. | 10:56 | 10:54 | 10:52 | 10:49 | 10:47 | 10:43 | 10:38 | 10:31 |
| MARS | MER. | JUP. | VEN. | SAT. | SUN | MOON | 12: 4 | 12: 4 | 12: 4 | 12: 4 | 12: 4 | 12: 4 | 12: 4 | 12: 4 |
| SUN | MOON | MARS | MER. | JUP. | VEN. | SAT. | 1:12 | 1:14 | 1:16 | 1:19 | 1:21 | 1:25 | 1:30 | 1:37 |
| VEN. | SAT. | SUN | MOON | MARS | MER. | JUP. | 2:20 | 2:24 | 2:28 | 2:33 | 2:39 | 2:46 | 2:56 | 3:10 |
| MER. | JUP. | VEN. | SAT. | SUN | MOON | MARS | 3:28 | 3:34 | 3:40 | 3:48 | 3:56 | 4: 7 | 4:22 | 4:42 |
| MOON | MARS | MER. | JUP. | VEN. | SAT. | SUN | 4:36 | 4:44 | 4:53 | 5: 2 | 5:14 | 5:28 | 5:47 | 6:15 |
| SAT. | SUN | MOON | MARS | MER. | JUP. | VEN. | 5:45 | 5:54 | 6: 5 | 6:17 | 6:31 | 6:49 | 7:13 | 7:48 |

### NIGHT HOURS: SUNSET TO SUNRISE (LOCAL MEAN TIME)

| SUN. | MON. | TU. | WED. | TH. | FRI. | SAT. | LAT. 25° | LAT. 30° | LAT. 35° | LAT. 40° | LAT. 45° | LAT. 50° | LAT. 55° | LAT. 60° |
|---|---|---|---|---|---|---|---|---|---|---|---|---|---|---|
| JUP. | VEN. | SAT. | SUN | MOON | MARS | MER. | 6:53 | 7: 4 | 7:17 | 7:31 | 7:49 | 8:10 | 8:39 | 9:21 |
| MARS | MER. | JUP. | VEN. | SAT. | SUN | MOON | 7:45 | 7:54 | 8: 5 | 8:17 | 8:31 | 8:49 | 9:13 | 9:48 |
| SUN | MOON | MARS | MER. | JUP. | VEN. | SAT. | 8:36 | 8:44 | 8:53 | 9: 2 | 9:14 | 9:28 | 9:47 | 10:15 |
| VEN. | SAT. | SUN | MOON | MARS | MER. | JUP. | 9:28 | 9:34 | 9:40 | 9:48 | 9:56 | 10: 7 | 10:22 | 10:42 |
| MER. | JUP. | VEN. | SAT. | SUN | MOON | MARS | 10:20 | 10:24 | 10:28 | 10:33 | 10:39 | 10:46 | 10:56 | 11:10 |
| MOON | MARS | MER. | JUP. | VEN. | SAT. | SUN | 11:12 | 11:14 | 11:16 | 11:19 | 11:21 | 11:25 | 11:30 | 11:37 |
| SAT. | SUN | MOON | MARS | MER. | JUP. | VEN. | 12: 4 | 12: 4 | 12: 4 | 12: 4 | 12: 4 | 12: 4 | 12: 4 | 12: 4 |
| JUP. | VEN. | SAT. | SUN | MOON | MARS | MER. | 12:56 | 12:54 | 12:52 | 12:49 | 12:47 | 12:43 | 12:38 | 12:31 |
| MARS | MER. | JUP. | VEN. | SAT. | SUN | MOON | 1:48 | 1:44 | 1:40 | 1:35 | 1:29 | 1:22 | 1:12 | 12:58 |
| SUN | MOON | MARS | MER. | JUP. | VEN. | SAT. | 2:40 | 2:34 | 2:28 | 2:20 | 2:12 | 2: 1 | 1:47 | 1:46 |
| VEN. | SAT. | SUN | MOON | MARS | MER. | JUP. | 3:32 | 3:24 | 3:16 | 3: 6 | 2:54 | 2:40 | 2:21 | 1:53 |
| MER. | JUP. | VEN. | SAT. | SUN | MOON | MARS | 4:23 | 4:14 | 4: 3 | 3:51 | 3:37 | 3:19 | 2:55 | 2:20 |

# JULY 1 TO 15, ANY YEAR

## DAY HOURS: SUNRISE TO SUNSET (LOCAL MEAN TIME)

| SUN. | MON. | TU. | WED. | TH. | FRI. | SAT. | LAT. 25° | LAT. 30° | LAT. 35° | LAT. 40° | LAT. 45° | LAT. 50° | LAT. 55° | LAT. 60° |
|---|---|---|---|---|---|---|---|---|---|---|---|---|---|---|
| SUN | MOON | MARS | MER. | JUP. | VEN. | SAT. | 5:24 | 5:13 | 5: 1 | 4:43 | 4:27 | 4: 6 | 3:40 | 3: 1 |
| VEN. | SAT. | SUN | MOON | MARS | MER. | JUP. | 6:32 | 6:23 | 6:13 | 5:57 | 5:44 | 5:26 | 5: 4 | 4:32 |
| MER. | JUP. | VEN. | SAT. | SUN | MOON | MARS | 7:39 | 7:32 | 7:24 | 7:11 | 7: 0 | 6:47 | 6:29 | 6: 3 |
| MOON | MARS | MER. | JUP. | VEN. | SAT. | SUN | 8:47 | 8:41 | 8:35 | 8:25 | 8:17 | 8: 7 | 7:53 | 7:34 |
| SAT. | SUN | MOON | MARS | MER. | JUP. | VEN. | 9:54 | 9:50 | 9:46 | 9:39 | 9:33 | 9:27 | 9:18 | 9: 5 |
| JUP. | VEN. | SAT. | SUN | MOON | MARS | MER. | 11: 1 | 11: 0 | 10:58 | 10:53 | 10:50 | 10:47 | 10:42 | 10:36 |
| MARS | MER. | JUP. | VEN. | SAT. | SUN | MOON | 12: 9 | 12: 9 | 12: 9 | 12: 7 | 12: 7 | 12: 7 | 12: 7 | 12: 6 |
| SUN | MOON | MARS | MER. | JUP. | VEN. | SAT. | 1:16 | 1:18 | 1:20 | 1:21 | 1:23 | 1:27 | 1:31 | 1:37 |
| VEN. | SAT. | SUN | MOON | MARS | MER. | JUP. | 2:24 | 2:27 | 2:31 | 2:35 | 2:40 | 2:47 | 2:56 | 3: 8 |
| MER. | JUP. | VEN. | SAT. | SUN | MOON | MARS | 3:31 | 3:36 | 3:43 | 3:48 | 3:57 | 4: 7 | 4:20 | 4:39 |
| MOON | MARS | MER. | JUP. | VEN. | SAT. | SUN | 4:39 | 4:46 | 4:54 | 5: 2 | 5:13 | 5:27 | 5:45 | 6:10 |
| SAT. | SUN | MOON | MARS | MER. | JUP. | VEN. | 5:46 | 5:55 | 6: 5 | 6:16 | 6:30 | 6:47 | 7: 9 | 7:41 |

## NIGHT HOURS: SUNSET TO SUNRISE (LOCAL MEAN TIME)

| SUN. | MON. | TU. | WED. | TH. | FRI. | SAT. | LAT. 25° | LAT. 30° | LAT. 35° | LAT. 40° | LAT. 45° | LAT. 50° | LAT. 55° | LAT. 60° |
|---|---|---|---|---|---|---|---|---|---|---|---|---|---|---|
| JUP. | VEN. | SAT. | SUN | MOON | MARS | MER. | 6:53 | 7: 4 | 7:16 | 7:30 | 7:47 | 8: 7 | 8:34 | 9:12 |
| MARS | MER. | JUP. | VEN. | SAT. | SUN | MOON | 7:46 | 7:55 | 8: 5 | 8:16 | 8:30 | 8:47 | 9: 9 | 9:41 |
| SUN | MOON | MARS | MER. | JUP. | VEN. | SAT. | 8:39 | 8:46 | 8:54 | 9: 2 | 9:13 | 9:27 | 9:45 | 10:10 |
| VEN. | SAT. | SUN | MOON | MARS | MER. | JUP. | 9:31 | 9:36 | 9:43 | 9:48 | 9:57 | 10: 7 | 10:20 | 10:39 |
| MER. | JUP. | VEN. | SAT. | SUN | MOON | MARS | 10:24 | 10:27 | 10:31 | 10:35 | 10:40 | 10:47 | 10:56 | 11: 8 |
| MOON | MARS | MER. | JUP. | VEN. | SAT. | SUN | 11:16 | 11:18 | 11:20 | 11:21 | 11:23 | 11:27 | 11:31 | 11:37 |
| SAT. | SUN | MOON | MARS | MER. | JUP. | VEN. | 12: 9 | 12: 9 | 12: 9 | 12: 7 | 12: 7 | 12: 7 | 12: 7 | 12: 6 |
| JUP. | VEN. | SAT. | SUN | MOON | MARS | MER. | 1: 1 | 1: 0 | 12:58 | 12:53 | 12:50 | 12:47 | 12:42 | 12:36 |
| MARS | MER. | JUP. | VEN. | SAT. | SUN | MOON | 1:54 | 1:50 | 1:46 | 1:39 | 1:33 | 1:27 | 1:18 | 1: 5 |
| SUN | MOON | MARS | MER. | JUP. | VEN. | SAT. | 2:47 | 2:42 | 2:35 | 2:25 | 2:17 | 2: 7 | 1:53 | 1:34 |
| VEN. | SAT. | SUN | MOON | MARS | MER. | JUP. | 3:39 | 3:32 | 3:24 | 3:11 | 3: 0 | 2:47 | 2:29 | 2: 3 |
| MER. | JUP. | VEN. | SAT. | SUN | MOON | MARS | 4:32 | 4:23 | 4:13 | 3:57 | 3:44 | 3:26 | 3: 4 | 2:32 |

# JULY 16 TO 31, ANY YEAR

## DAY HOURS: SUNRISE TO SUNSET (LOCAL MEAN TIME)

| SUN. | MON. | TU. | WED. | TH. | FRI. | SAT. | LAT. 25° | LAT. 30° | LAT. 35° | LAT. 40° | LAT. 45° | LAT. 50° | LAT. 55° | LAT. 60° |
|---|---|---|---|---|---|---|---|---|---|---|---|---|---|---|
| SUN | MOON | MARS | MER. | JUP. | VEN. | SAT. | 5:31 | 5:21 | 5:11 | 4:59 | 4:44 | 4:27 | 4: 4 | 3:28 |
| VEN. | SAT. | SUN | MOON | MARS | MER. | JUP. | 6:37 | 6:30 | 6:21 | 6:11 | 5:59 | 5:44 | 5:25 | 4:55 |
| MER. | JUP. | VEN. | SAT. | SUN | MOON | MARS | 7:44 | 7:38 | 7:31 | 7:22 | 7:13 | 7: 1 | 6:46 | 6:21 |
| MOON | MARS | MER. | JUP. | VEN. | SAT. | SUN | 8:51 | 8:46 | 8:40 | 8:34 | 8:27 | 8:18 | 8: 7 | 7:48 |
| SAT. | SUN | MOON | MARS | MER. | JUP. | VEN. | 9:57 | 9:54 | 9:50 | 9:46 | 9:41 | 9:36 | 9:28 | 9:15 |
| JUP. | VEN. | SAT. | SUN | MOON | MARS | MER. | 11: 4 | 11: 2 | 11: 0 | 10:58 | 10:56 | 10:53 | 10:49 | 10:41 |
| MARS | MER. | JUP. | VEN. | SAT. | SUN | MOON | 12:10 | 12:10 | 12:10 | 12:10 | 12:10 | 12:10 | 12:10 | 12: 8 |
| SUN | MOON | MARS | MER. | JUP. | VEN. | SAT. | 1:17 | 1:18 | 1:20 | 1:22 | 1:24 | 1:27 | 1:31 | 1 34 |
| VEN. | SAT. | SUN | MOON | MARS | MER. | JUP. | 2:23 | 2:26 | 2:30 | 2:34 | 2:39 | 2:44 | 2:52 | 3: 1 |
| MER. | JUP. | VEN. | SAT. | SUN | MOON | MARS | 3:30 | 3:35 | 3:40 | 3:46 | 3:53 | 4: 2 | 4:13 | 4:27 |
| MOON | MARS | MER. | JUP. | VEN. | SAT. | SUN | 4:36 | 4:43 | 4:50 | 4:58 | 5: 7 | 5:19 | 5:34 | 5:54 |
| SAT. | SUN | MOON | MARS | MER. | JUP. | VEN. | 5:43 | 5:51 | 6: 0 | 6:10 | 6:22 | 6:36 | 6:55 | 7:20 |

## NIGHT HOURS: SUNSET TO SUNRISE (LOCAL MEAN TIME)

| SUN. | MON. | TU. | WED. | TH. | FRI. | SAT. | LAT. 25° | LAT. 30° | LAT. 35° | LAT. 40° | LAT. 45° | LAT. 50° | LAT. 55° | LAT. 60° |
|---|---|---|---|---|---|---|---|---|---|---|---|---|---|---|
| JUP. | VEN. | SAT. | SUN | MOON | MARS | MER. | 6:50 | 6:59 | 7:10 | 7:22 | 7:36 | 7:53 | 8:16 | 8:47 |
| MARS | MER. | JUP. | VEN. | SAT. | SUN | MOON | 7:43 | 7:51 | 8: 0 | 8:10 | 8:22 | 8:36 | 8:55 | 9:20 |
| SUN | MOON | MARS | MER. | JUP. | VEN. | SAT. | 8:36 | 8:43 | 8:50 | 8:58 | 9: 7 | 9:19 | 9:34 | 9:54 |
| VEN. | SAT. | SUN | MOON | MARS | MER. | JUP. | 9:30 | 9:35 | 9:40 | 9:46 | 9:53 | 10: 2 | 10:13 | 10:27 |
| MER. | JUP. | VEN. | SAT. | SUN | MOON | MARS | 10:23 | 10:26 | 10:30 | 10:34 | 10:39 | 10:44 | 10:52 | 11: 1 |
| MOON | MARS | MER. | JUP. | VEN. | SAT. | SUN | 11:17 | 11:18 | 11:20 | 11:22 | 11:24 | 11:27 | 11:31 | 11:34 |
| SAT. | SUN | MOON | MARS | MER. | JUP. | VEN. | 12:10 | 12:10 | 12:10 | 12:10 | 12:10 | 12:10 | 12:10 | 12: 8 |
| JUP. | VEN. | SAT. | SUN | MOON | MARS | MER. | 1: 4 | 1: 2 | 1: 0 | 12:58 | 12:56 | 12:53 | 12:49 | 12:41 |
| MARS | MER. | JUP. | VEN. | SAT. | SUN | MOON | 1:57 | 1:54 | 1:50 | 1:46 | 1:41 | 1:36 | 1:28 | 1:15 |
| SUN | MOON | MARS | MER. | JUP. | VEN. | SAT. | 2:51 | 2:46 | 2:40 | 2:34 | 2:27 | 2:18 | 2: 7 | 1:48 |
| VEN. | SAT. | SUN | MOON | MARS | MER. | JUP. | 3:44 | 3:38 | 3:31 | 3:22 | 3:13 | 3: 1 | 2:46 | 2:21 |
| MER. | JUP. | VEN. | SAT. | SUN | MOON | MARS | 4:37 | 4:30 | 4:21 | 4:11 | 3:59 | 3:44 | 3:25 | 2:55 |

## DAY HOURS: SUNRISE TO SUNSET (LOCAL MEAN TIME)

| SUN. | MON. | TU. | WED. | TH. | FRI. | SAT. | LAT. 25° | LAT. 30° | LAT. 35° | LAT. 40° | LAT. 45° | LAT. 50° | LAT. 55° | LAT. 60° |
|---|---|---|---|---|---|---|---|---|---|---|---|---|---|---|
| SUN | MOON | MARS | MER. | JUP. | VEN. | SAT. | 5:38 | 5:31 | 5:23 | 5:13 | 5: 2 | 4:48 | 4:31 | 4: 8 |
| VEN. | SAT. | SUN | MOON | MARS | MER. | JUP. | 6:44 | 6:37 | 6:30 | 6:22 | 6:13 | 6: 2 | 5:47 | 5:28 |
| MER. | JUP. | VEN. | SAT. | SUN | MOON | MARS | 7:49 | 7:44 | 7:38 | 7:32 | 7:24 | 7:15 | 7: 4 | 6:48 |
| MOON | MARS | MER. | JUP. | VEN. | SAT. | SUN | 8:54 | 8:50 | 8:46 | 8:41 | 8:36 | 8:29 | 8:20 | 8: 8 |
| SAT. | SUN | MOON | MARS | MER. | JUP. | VEN. | 9:59 | 9:57 | 9:54 | 9:51 | 9:47 | 9:42 | 9:36 | 9:29 |
| JUP. | VEN. | SAT. | SUN | MOON | MARS | MER. | 11: 4 | 11: 3 | 11: 2 | 11: 0 | 10:58 | 10:56 | 10:53 | 10:49 |
| MARS | MER. | JUP. | VEN. | SAT. | SUN | MOON | 12: 9 | 12: 9 | 12: 9 | 12: 9 | 12: 9 | 12: 9 | 12: 9 | 12: 9 |
| SUN | MOON | MARS | MER. | JUP. | VEN. | SAT. | 1:15 | 1:16 | 1:17 | 1:19 | 1:20 | 1:23 | 1:25 | 1:29 |
| VEN. | SAT. | SUN | MOON | MARS | MER. | JUP. | 2:20 | 2:22 | 2:25 | 2:28 | 2:32 | 2:36 | 2:42 | 2:49 |
| MER. | JUP. | VEN. | SAT. | SUN | MOON | MARS | 3:25 | 3:29 | 3:33 | 3:37 | 3:43 | 3:50 | 3:58 | 4: 9 |
| MOON | MARS | MER. | JUP. | VEN. | SAT. | SUN | 4:30 | 4:35 | 4:41 | 4:47 | 4:54 | 5: 3 | 5:14 | 5:29 |
| SAT. | SUN | MOON | MARS | MER. | JUP. | VEN. | 5:35 | 5:41 | 5:48 | 5:56 | 6: 5 | 6:16 | 6:30 | 6:49 |

## NIGHT HOURS: SUNSET TO SUNRISE (LOCAL MEAN TIME)

| SUN. | MON. | TU. | WED. | TH. | FRI. | SAT. |
|---|---|---|---|---|---|---|
| JUP. | VEN. | SAT. | SUN | MOON | MARS | MER. |
| MARS | MER. | JUP. | VEN. | SAT. | SUN | MOON |
| SUN | MOON | MARS | MER. | JUP. | VEN. | SAT. |
| VEN. | SAT. | SUN | MOON | MARS | MER. | JUP. |
| MER. | JUP. | VEN. | SAT. | SUN | MOON | MARS |
| MOON | MARS | MER. | JUP. | VEN. | SAT. | SUN |
| SAT. | SUN | MOON | MARS | MER. | JUP. | VEN. |
| JUP. | VEN. | SAT. | SUN | MOON | MARS | MER. |
| MARS | MER. | JUP. | VEN. | SAT. | SUN | MOON |
| SUN | MOON | MARS | MER. | JUP. | VEN. | SAT. |
| VEN. | SAT. | SUN | MOON | MARS | MER. | JUP. |
| MER. | JUP. | VEN. | SAT. | SUN | MOON | MARS |

# AUGUST 16 TO 31, ANY YEAR

## DAY HOURS: SUNRISE TO SUNSET (LOCAL MEAN TIME)

| SUN. | MON. | TU. | WED. | TH. | FRI. | SAT. | LAT. 25° | LAT. 30° | LAT. 35° | LAT. 40° | LAT. 45° | LAT. 50° | LAT. 55° | LAT. 60° |
|---|---|---|---|---|---|---|---|---|---|---|---|---|---|---|
| SUN | MOON | MARS | MER. | JUP. | VEN. | SAT. | 5:45 | 5:40 | 5:34 | 5:27 | 5:19 | 5:10 | 4:59 | 4:44 |
| VEN. | SAT. | SUN | MOON | MARS | MER. | JUP. | 6:48 | 6:44 | 6:39 | 6:34 | 6:27 | 6:20 | 6:10 | 5:57 |
| MER. | JUP. | VEN. | SAT. | SUN | MOON | MARS | 7:52 | 7:49 | 7:45 | 7:40 | 7:35 | 7:29 | 7:21 | 7:11 |
| MOON | MARS | MER. | JUP. | VEN. | SAT. | SUN | 8:56 | 8:53 | 8:50 | 8:47 | 8:43 | 8:38 | 8:32 | 8:25 |
| SAT. | SUN | MOON | MARS | MER. | JUP. | VEN. | 9:59 | 9:57 | 9:55 | 9:53 | 9:51 | 9:47 | 9:44 | 9:38 |
| JUP. | VEN. | SAT. | SUN | MOON | MARS | MER. | 11: 3 | 11: 2 | 11: 1 | 11: 0 | 10:58 | 10:57 | 10:55 | 10:52 |
| MARS | MER. | JUP. | VEN. | SAT. | SUN | MOON | 12: 6 | 12: 6 | 12: 6 | 12: 6 | 12: 6 | 12: 6 | 12: 6 | 12: 6 |
| SUN | MOON | MARS | MER. | JUP. | VEN. | SAT. | 1:10 | 1:11 | 1:12 | 1:13 | 1:14 | 1:15 | 1:17 | 1:20 |
| VEN. | SAT. | SUN | MOON | MARS | MER. | JUP. | 2:14 | 2:15 | 2:17 | 2:19 | 2:22 | 2:25 | 2:28 | 2:33 |
| MER. | JUP. | VEN. | SAT. | SUN | MOON | MARS | 3:17 | 3:20 | 3:23 | 3:26 | 3:30 | 3:34 | 3:40 | 3:47 |
| MOON | MARS | MER. | JUP. | VEN. | SAT. | SUN | 4:21 | 4:24 | 4:28 | 4:32 | 4:37 | 4:43 | 4:51 | 5: 1 |
| SAT. | SUN | MOON | MARS | MER. | JUP. | VEN. | 5:25 | 5:29 | 5:34 | 5:39 | 5:45 | 5:53 | 6: 2 | 6:14 |

## NIGHT HOURS: SUNSET TO SUNRISE (LOCAL MEAN TIME)

| SUN. | MON. | TU. | WED. | TH. | FRI. | SAT. | LAT. 25° | LAT. 30° | LAT. 35° | LAT. 40° | LAT. 45° | LAT. 50° | LAT. 55° | LAT. 60° |
|---|---|---|---|---|---|---|---|---|---|---|---|---|---|---|
| JUP. | VEN. | SAT. | SUN | MOON | MARS | MER. | 6:28 | 6:33 | 6:39 | 6:45 | 6:53 | 7: 2 | 7:13 | 7:28 |
| MARS | MER. | JUP. | VEN. | SAT. | SUN | MOON | 7:25 | 7:29 | 7:34 | 7:39 | 7:45 | 7:53 | 8: 2 | 8:14 |
| SUN | MOON | MARS | MER. | JUP. | VEN. | SAT. | 8:21 | 8:24 | 8:28 | 8:32 | 8:37 | 8:43 | 8:51 | 9: 1 |
| VEN. | SAT. | SUN | MOON | MARS | MER. | JUP. | 9:17 | 9:20 | 9:23 | 9:26 | 9:30 | 9:34 | 9:40 | 9:47 |
| MER. | JUP. | VEN. | SAT. | SUN | MOON | MARS | 10:14 | 10:15 | 10:17 | 10:19 | 10:22 | 10:25 | 10:28 | 10:33 |
| MOON | MARS | MER. | JUP. | VEN. | SAT. | SUN | 11:10 | 11:11 | 11:12 | 11:13 | 11:14 | 11:15 | 11:17 | 11:20 |
| SAT. | SUN | MOON | MARS | MER. | JUP. | VEN. | 12: 6 | 12: 6 | 12: 6 | 12: 6 | 12: 6 | 12: 6 | 12: 6 | 12: 6 |
| JUP. | VEN. | SAT. | SUN | MOON | MARS | MER. | 1: 3 | 1: 2 | 1: 1 | 1: 0 | 12:58 | 12:57 | 12:55 | 12:52 |
| MARS | MER. | JUP. | VEN. | SAT. | SUN | MOON | 1:59 | 1:57 | 1:55 | 1:53 | 1:51 | 1:47 | 1:44 | 1:38 |
| SUN | MOON | MARS | MER. | JUP. | VEN. | SAT. | 2:56 | 2:53 | 2:50 | 2:47 | 2:43 | 2:38 | 2:32 | 2:25 |
| VEN. | SAT. | SUN | MOON | MARS | MER. | JUP. | 3:52 | 3:49 | 3:45 | 3:40 | 3:35 | 3:29 | 3:21 | 3:11 |
| MER. | JUP. | VEN. | SAT. | SUN | MOON | MARS | 4:48 | 4:44 | 4:39 | 4:34 | 4:27 | 4:20 | 4:10 | 3:57 |

### DAY HOURS: SUNRISE TO SUNSET (LOCAL MEAN TIME)

| SUN. | MON. | TU. | WED. | TH. | FRI. | SAT. | LAT. 25° | LAT. 30° | LAT. 35° | LAT. 40° | LAT. 45° | LAT. 50° | LAT. 55° | LAT. 60° |
|---|---|---|---|---|---|---|---|---|---|---|---|---|---|---|
| SUN | MOON | MARS | MER. | JUP. | VEN. | SAT. | 5:51 | 5:48 | 5:45 | 5:42 | 5:38 | 5:34 | 5:28 | 5:21 |
| VEN. | SAT. | SUN | MOON | MARS | MER. | JUP. | 6:53 | 6:50 | 6:48 | 6:45 | 6:42 | 6:38 | 6:34 | 6:28 |
| MER. | JUP. | VEN. | SAT. | SUN | MOON | MARS | 7:54 | 7:53 | 7:51 | 7:49 | 7:46 | 7:43 | 7:39 | 7:34 |
| MOON | MARS | MER. | JUP. | VEN. | SAT. | SUN | 8:56 | 8:55 | 8:53 | 8:52 | 8:50 | 8:48 | 8:45 | 8:41 |
| SAT. | SUN | MOON | MARS | MER. | JUP. | VEN. | 9:58 | 9:57 | 9:56 | 9:55 | 9:54 | 9:52 | 9:50 | 9:48 |
| JUP. | VEN. | SAT. | SUN | MOON | MARS | MER. | 11: 0 | 10:59 | 10:59 | 10:58 | 10:57 | 10:56 | 10:56 | 10:54 |
| MARS | MER. | JUP. | VEN. | SAT. | SUN | MOON | 12: 2 | 12: 1 | 12: 1 | 12: 1 | 12: 1 | 12: 1 | 12: 1 | 12: 1 |
| SUN | MOON | MARS | MER. | JUP. | VEN. | SAT. | 1: 3 | 1: 4 | 1: 4 | 1: 5 | 1: 5 | 1: 6 | 1: 7 | 1: 8 |
| VEN. | SAT. | SUN | MOON | MARS | MER. | JUP. | 2: 5 | 2: 6 | 2: 7 | 2: 8 | 2: 9 | 2:10 | 2:12 | 2:14 |
| MER. | JUP. | VEN. | SAT. | SUN | MOON | MARS | 3: 7 | 3: 8 | 3: 9 | 3:11 | 3:13 | 3:15 | 3:18 | 3:21 |
| MOON | MARS | MER. | JUP. | VEN. | SAT. | SUN | 4: 9 | 4:10 | 4:12 | 4:14 | 4:17 | 4:20 | 4:23 | 4:28 |
| SAT. | SUN | MOON | MARS | MER. | JUP. | VEN. | 5:10 | 5:13 | 5:15 | 5:17 | 5:20 | 5:24 | 5:29 | 5:34 |

### NIGHT HOURS: SUNSET TO SUNRISE (LOCAL MEAN TIME)

| SUN. | MON. | TU. | WED. | TH. | FRI. | SAT. | LAT. 25° | LAT. 30° | LAT. 35° | LAT. 40° | LAT. 45° | LAT. 50° | LAT. 55° | LAT. 60° |
|---|---|---|---|---|---|---|---|---|---|---|---|---|---|---|
| JUP. | VEN. | SAT. | SUN | MOON | MARS | MER. | 6:12 | 6:15 | 6:17 | 6:21 | 6:24 | 6:29 | 6:34 | 6:41 |
| MARS | MER. | JUP. | VEN. | SAT. | SUN | MOON | 7:10 | 7:13 | 7:15 | 7:17 | 7:20 | 7:24 | 7:29 | 7:34 |
| SUN | MOON | MARS | MER. | JUP. | VEN. | SAT. | 8: 9 | 8:10 | 8:12 | 8:14 | 8:17 | 8:20 | 8:23 | 8:28 |
| VEN. | SAT. | SUN | MOON | MARS | MER. | JUP. | 9: 7 | 9: 8 | 9: 9 | 9:11 | 9:13 | 9:15 | 9:18 | 9:21 |
| MER. | JUP. | VEN. | SAT. | SUN | MOON | MARS | 10: 5 | 10: 6 | 10: 7 | 10: 8 | 10: 9 | 10:10 | 10:12 | 10:14 |
| MOON | MARS | MER. | JUP. | VEN. | SAT. | SUN | 11: 3 | 11: 3 | 11: 4 | 11: 5 | 11: 5 | 11: 6 | 11: 7 | 11: 8 |
| SAT. | SUN | MOON | MARS | MER. | JUP. | VEN. | 12: 2 | 12: 1 | 12: 1 | 12: 1 | 12: 1 | 12: 1 | 12: 1 | 12: 1 |
| JUP. | VEN. | SAT. | SUN | MOON | MARS | MER. | 1: 0 | 12:59 | 12:59 | 12:58 | 12:57 | 12:57 | 12:56 | 12:54 |
| MARS | MER. | JUP. | VEN. | SAT. | SUN | MOON | 1:58 | 1:57 | 1:56 | 1:55 | 1:54 | 1:52 | 1:50 | 1:48 |
| SUN | MOON | MARS | MER. | JUP. | VEN. | SAT. | 2:56 | 2:55 | 2:53 | 2:52 | 2:50 | 2:48 | 2:45 | 2:41 |
| VEN. | SAT. | SUN | MOON | MARS | MER. | JUP. | 3:54 | 3:53 | 3:51 | 3:49 | 3:46 | 3:43 | 3:39 | 3:34 |
| MER. | JUP. | VEN. | SAT. | SUN | MOON | MARS | 4:53 | 4:50 | 4:48 | 4:45 | 4:42 | 4:38 | 4:34 | 4:28 |

## SEPTEMBER 16 TO 30, ANY YEAR

### DAY HOURS: SUNRISE TO SUNSET (LOCAL MEAN TIME)

| SUN. | MON. | TU. | WED. | TH. | FRI. | SAT. | LAT. 25° | LAT. 30° | LAT. 35° | LAT. 40° | LAT. 45° | LAT. 50° | LAT. 55° | LAT. 60° |
|---|---|---|---|---|---|---|---|---|---|---|---|---|---|---|
| SUN | MOON | MARS | MER. | JUP. | VEN. | SAT. | 5:52 | 5:52 | 5:52 | 5:52 | 5:52 | 5:52 | 5:52 | 5:52 |
| VEN. | SAT. | SUN | MOON | MARS | MER. | JUP. | 6:52 | 6:52 | 6:52 | 6:52 | 6:52 | 6:52 | 6:52 | 6:52 |
| MER. | JUP. | VEN. | SAT. | SUN | MOON | MARS | 7:52 | 7:52 | 7:52 | 7:52 | 7:52 | 7:28 | 7:52 | 7:52 |
| MOON | MARS | MER. | JUP. | VEN. | SAT. | SUN | 8:52 | 8:52 | 8:52 | 8:52 | 8:52 | 8:52 | 8:52 | 8:52 |
| SAT. | SUN | MOON | MARS | MER. | JUP. | VEN. | 9:52 | 9:52 | 9:52 | 9:52 | 9:52 | 9:52 | 9:52 | 9:52 |
| JUP. | VEN. | SAT. | SUN | MOON | MARS | MER. | 10:52 | 10:52 | 10:52 | 10:52 | 10:52 | 10:52 | 10:52 | 10:52 |
| MARS | MER. | JUP. | VEN. | SAT. | SUN | MOON | 11:52 | 11:52 | 11:52 | 11:52 | 11:52 | 11:52 | 11:52 | 11:52 |
| SUN | MOON | MARS | MER. | JUP. | VEN. | SAT. | 12:52 | 12:52 | 12:52 | 12:52 | 12:52 | 12:52 | 12:52 | 12:52 |
| VEN. | SAT. | SUN | MOON | MARS | MER. | JUP. | 1:52 | 1:52 | 1:52 | 1:52 | 1:52 | 1:52 | 1:52 | 1:52 |
| MER. | JUP. | VEN. | SAT. | SUN | MOON | MARS | 2:52 | 2:52 | 2:52 | 2:52 | 2:52 | 2:52 | 2:52 | 2:52 |
| MOON | MARS | MER. | JUP. | VEN. | SAT. | SUN | 3:52 | 3:52 | 3:52 | 3:52 | 3:52 | 3:52 | 3:52 | 3:52 |
| SAT. | SUN | MOON | MARS | MER. | JUP. | VEN. | 4:52 | 4:52 | 4:52 | 4:52 | 4:52 | 4:52 | 4:52 | 4:52 |

### NIGHT HOURS: SUNSET TO SUNRISE (LOCAL MEAN TIME)

| SUN. | MON. | TU. | WED. | TH. | FRI. | SAT. | LAT. 25° | LAT. 30° | LAT. 35° | LAT. 40° | LAT. 45° | LAT. 50° | LAT. 55° | LAT. 60° |
|---|---|---|---|---|---|---|---|---|---|---|---|---|---|---|
| JUP. | VEN. | SAT. | SUN | MOON | MARS | MER. | 5:52 | 5:52 | 5:52 | 5:52 | 5:52 | 5:52 | 5:52 | 5:52 |
| MARS | MER. | JUP. | VEN. | SAT. | SUN | MOON | 6:52 | 6:52 | 6:52 | 6:52 | 6:52 | 6:52 | 6:52 | 6:52 |
| SUN | MOON | MARS | MER. | JUP. | VEN. | SAT. | 7:52 | 7:52 | 7:52 | 7:52 | 7:52 | 7:52 | 7:52 | 7:52 |
| VEN. | SAT. | SUN | MOON | MARS | MER. | JUP. | 8:52 | 8:52 | 8:52 | 8:52 | 8:52 | 8:52 | 8:52 | 8:52 |
| MER. | JUP. | VEN. | SAT. | SUN | MOON | MARS | 9:52 | 9:52 | 9:52 | 9:52 | 9:52 | 9:52 | 9:52 | 9:52 |
| MOON | MARS | MER. | JUP. | VEN. | SAT. | SUN | 10:52 | 10:52 | 10:52 | 10:52 | 10:52 | 10:52 | 10:52 | 10:52 |
| SAT. | SUN | MOON | MARS | MER. | JUP. | VEN. | 11:52 | 11:52 | 11:52 | 11:52 | 11:52 | 11:52 | 11:52 | 11:52 |
| JUP. | VEN. | SAT. | SUN | MOON | MARS | MER. | 12:52 | 12:52 | 12:52 | 12:52 | 12:52 | 12:52 | 12:52 | 12:52 |
| MARS | MER. | JUP. | VEN. | SAT. | SUN | MOON | 1:52 | 1:52 | 1:52 | 1:52 | 1:52 | 1:52 | 1:52 | 1:52 |
| SUN | MOON | MARS | MER. | JUP. | VEN. | SAT. | 2:52 | 2:52 | 2:52 | 2:52 | 2:52 | 2:52 | 2:52 | 2:52 |
| VEN. | SAT. | SUN | MOON | MARS | MER. | JUP. | 3:52 | 3:52 | 3:52 | 3:52 | 3:52 | 3:52 | 3:52 | 3:52 |
| MER. | JUP. | VEN. | SAT. | SUN | MOON | MARS | 4:52 | 4:52 | 4:52 | 4:52 | 4:52 | 4:52 | 4:52 | 4:52 |

# OCTOBER 1 TO 15, ANY YEAR

## DAY HOURS: SUNRISE TO SUNSET (LOCAL MEAN TIME)

| SUN. | MON. | TU. | WED. | TH. | FRI. | SAT. | LAT. 25° | LAT. 30° | LAT. 35° | LAT. 40° | LAT. 45° | LAT. 50° | LAT. 55° | LAT. 60° |
|---|---|---|---|---|---|---|---|---|---|---|---|---|---|---|
| SUN | MOON | MARS | MER. | JUP. | VEN. | SAT. | 5:58 | 6: 1 | 6: 4 | 6: 7 | 6:11 | 6:15 | 6:21 | 6:28 |
| VEN. | SAT. | SUN | MOON | MARS | MER. | JUP. | 6:57 | 6:59 | 7: 1 | 7: 4 | 7: 7 | 7:11 | 7:15 | 7:21 |
| MER. | JUP. | VEN. | SAT. | SUN | MOON | MARS | 7:55 | 7:57 | 7:58 | 8: 1 | 8: 3 | 8: 6 | 8:10 | 8:14 |
| MOON | MARS | MER. | JUP. | VEN. | SAT. | SUN | 8:53 | 8:54 | 8:56 | 8:57 | 8:59 | 9: 1 | 9: 4 | 9: 8 |
| SAT. | SUN | MOON | MARS | MER. | JUP. | VEN. | 9:51 | 9:52 | 9:53 | 9:54 | 9:55 | 9:57 | 9:58 | 10: 1 |
| JUP. | VEN. | SAT. | SUN | MOON | MARS | MER. | 10:49 | 10:50 | 10:51 | 10:51 | 10:51 | 10:52 | 10:53 | 10:54 |
| MARS | MER. | JUP. | VEN. | SAT. | SUN | MOON | 11:47 | 11:47 | 11:47 | 11:47 | 11:47 | 11:47 | 11:47 | 11:47 |
| SUN | MOON | MARS | MER. | JUP. | VEN. | SAT. | 12:46 | 12:45 | 12:45 | 12:44 | 12:43 | 12:43 | 12:42 | 12:40 |
| VEN. | SAT. | SUN | MOON | MARS | MER. | JUP. | 1:44 | 1:43 | 1:42 | 1:41 | 1:39 | 1:38 | 1:36 | 1:33 |
| MER. | JUP. | VEN. | SAT. | SUN | MOON | MARS | 2:42 | 2:41 | 2:39 | 2:37 | 2:36 | 2:33 | 2:30 | 2:27 |
| MOON | MARS | MER. | JUP. | VEN. | SAT. | SUN | 3:40 | 3:38 | 3:36 | 3:34 | 3:32 | 3:29 | 3:25 | 3:20 |
| SAT. | SUN | MOON | MARS | MER. | JUP. | VEN. | 4:38 | 4:36 | 4:34 | 4:31 | 4:28 | 4:24 | 4:19 | 4:13 |

## NIGHT HOURS: SUNSET TO SUNRISE (LOCAL MEAN TIME)

| SUN. | MON. | TU. | WED. | TH. | FRI. | SAT. | LAT. 25° | LAT. 30° | LAT. 35° | LAT. 40° | LAT. 45° | LAT. 50° | LAT. 55° | LAT. 60° |
|---|---|---|---|---|---|---|---|---|---|---|---|---|---|---|
| JUP. | VEN. | SAT. | SUN | MOON | MARS | MER. | 5:36 | 5:34 | 5:31 | 5:28 | 5:24 | 5:19 | 5:14 | 5: 6 |
| MARS | MER. | JUP. | VEN. | SAT. | SUN | MOON | 6:38 | 6:36 | 6:34 | 6:31 | 6:28 | 6:24 | 6:19 | 6:13 |
| SUN | MOON | MARS | MER. | JUP. | VEN. | SAT. | 7:40 | 7:38 | 7:36 | 7:34 | 7:32 | 7:29 | 7:25 | 7:20 |
| VEN. | SAT. | SUN | MOON | MARS | MER. | JUP. | 8:42 | 8:41 | 8:39 | 8:37 | 8:36 | 8:33 | 8:30 | 8:27 |
| MER. | JUP. | VEN. | SAT. | SUN | MOON | MARS | 9:44 | 9:43 | 9:42 | 9:41 | 9:39 | 9:38 | 9:36 | 9:33 |
| MOON | MARS | MER. | JUP. | VEN. | SAT. | SUN | 10:46 | 10:45 | 10:45 | 10:44 | 10:43 | 10:43 | 10:42 | 10:40 |
| SAT. | SUN | MOON | MARS | MER. | JUP. | VEN. | 11:47 | 11:47 | 11:47 | 11:47 | 11:47 | 11:47 | 11:47 | 11:47 |
| JUP. | VEN. | SAT. | SUN | MOON | MARS | MER. | 12:49 | 12:50 | 12:50 | 12:51 | 12:51 | 12:52 | 12:53 | 12:54 |
| MARS | MER. | JUP. | VEN. | SAT. | SUN | MOON | 1:51 | 1:52 | 1:53 | 1:54 | 1:55 | 1:57 | 1:58 | 2: 1 |
| SUN | MOON | MARS | MER. | JUP. | VEN. | SAT. | 2:53 | 2:54 | 2:56 | 2:57 | 2:59 | 3: 1 | 3: 4 | 3: 8 |
| VEN. | SAT. | SUN | MOON | MARS | MER. | JUP. | 3:55 | 3:57 | 3:58 | 4: 1 | 4: 3 | 4: 6 | 4:10 | 4:14 |
| MER. | JUP. | VEN. | SAT. | SUN | MOON | MARS | 4:57 | 4:59 | 5: 1 | 5: 4 | 5: 7 | 5:11 | 5:15 | 5:21 |

# OCTOBER 16 TO 31, ANY YEAR

## DAY HOURS: SUNRISE TO SUNSET (LOCAL MEAN TIME)

| SUN. | MON. | TU. | WED. | TH. | FRI. | SAT. | LAT. 25° | LAT. 30° | LAT. 35° | LAT. 40° | LAT. 45° | LAT. 50° | LAT. 55° | LAT. 60° |
|---|---|---|---|---|---|---|---|---|---|---|---|---|---|---|
| SUN | MOON | MARS | MER. | JUP. | VEN. | SAT. | 6: 6 | 6:11 | 6:17 | 6:23 | 6:31 | 6:40 | 6:51 | 7: 5 |
| VEN. | SAT. | SUN | MOON | MARS | MER. | JUP. | 7: 2 | 7: 6 | 7:11 | 7:17 | 7:23 | 7:30 | 7:40 | 7:52 |
| MER. | JUP. | VEN. | SAT. | SUN | MOON | MARS | 7:59 | 8: 2 | 8: 6 | 8:10 | 8:15 | 8:21 | 8:28 | 8:38 |
| MOON | MARS | MER. | JUP. | VEN. | SAT. | SUN | 8:55 | 8:58 | 9: 0 | 9: 4 | 9: 7 | 9:12 | 9:17 | 9:25 |
| SAT. | SUN | MOON | MARS | MER. | JUP. | VEN. | 9:51 | 9:53 | 9:55 | 9:57 | 10: 0 | 10: 3 | 10: 6 | 10:11 |
| JUP. | VEN. | SAT. | SUN | MOON | MARS | MER. | 10:48 | 10:49 | 10:50 | 10:51 | 10:52 | 10:53 | 10:55 | 10:57 |
| MARS | MER. | JUP. | VEN. | SAT. | SUN | MOON | 11:44 | 11:44 | 11:44 | 11:44 | 11:44 | 11:44 | 11:44 | 11:44 |
| SUN | MOON | MARS | MER. | JUP. | VEN. | SAT. | 12:41 | 12:40 | 12:39 | 12:38 | 12:36 | 12:35 | 12:33 | 12:30 |
| VEN. | SAT. | SUN | MOON | MARS | MER. | JUP. | 1:37 | 1:35 | 1:33 | 1:31 | 1:29 | 1:26 | 1:22 | 1:17 |
| MER. | JUP. | VEN. | SAT. | SUN | MOON | MARS | 2:33 | 2:31 | 2:28 | 2:25 | 2:21 | 2:16 | 2:11 | 2: 3 |
| MOON | MARS | MER. | JUP. | VEN. | SAT. | SUN | 3:30 | 3:26 | 3:23 | 3:18 | 3:13 | 3: 7 | 2:59 | 2:50 |
| SAT. | SUN | MOON | MARS | MER. | JUP. | VEN. | 4:26 | 4:22 | 4:17 | 4:12 | 4: 5 | 3:58 | 3:48 | 3:36 |

## NIGHT HOURS: SUNSET TO SUNRISE (LOCAL MEAN TIME)

| SUN. | MON. | TU. | WED. | TH. | FRI. | SAT. | LAT. 25° | LAT. 30° | LAT. 35° | LAT. 40° | LAT. 45° | LAT. 50° | LAT. 55° | LAT. 60° |
|---|---|---|---|---|---|---|---|---|---|---|---|---|---|---|
| JUP. | VEN. | SAT. | SUN | MOON | MARS | MER. | 5:23 | 5:18 | 5:12 | 5: 5 | 4:58 | 4:49 | 4:37 | 4:22 |
| MARS | MER. | JUP. | VEN. | SAT. | SUN | MOON | 6:26 | 6:22 | 6:17 | 6:12 | 6: 5 | 5:58 | 5:48 | 5:36 |
| SUN | MOON | MARS | MER. | JUP. | VEN. | SAT. | 7:30 | 7:26 | 7:23 | 7:18 | 7:13 | 7: 7 | 6:59 | 6:50 |
| VEN. | SAT. | SUN | MOON | MARS | MER. | JUP. | 8:33 | 8:31 | 8:28 | 8:25 | 8:21 | 8:16 | 8:11 | 8: 3 |
| MER. | JUP. | VEN. | SAT. | SUN | MOON | MARS | 9:37 | 9:35 | 9:33 | 9:31 | 9:29 | 9:26 | 9:22 | 9:17 |
| MOON | MARS | MER. | JUP. | VEN. | SAT. | SUN | 10:41 | 10:40 | 10:39 | 10:38 | 10:36 | 10:35 | 10:33 | 10:30 |
| SAT. | SUN | MOON | MARS | MER. | JUP. | VEN. | 11:44 | 11:44 | 11:44 | 11:44 | 11:44 | 11:44 | 11:44 | 11:44 |
| JUP. | VEN. | SAT. | SUN | MOON | MARS | MER. | 12:48 | 12:49 | 12:50 | 12:51 | 12:52 | 12:53 | 12:55 | 12:57 |
| MARS | MER. | JUP. | VEN. | SAT. | SUN | MOON | 1:51 | 1:53 | 1:55 | 1:57 | 2: 0 | 2: 3 | 2: 6 | 2:11 |
| SUN | MOON | MARS | MER. | JUP. | VEN. | SAT. | 2:55 | 2:58 | 3: 0 | 3: 4 | 3: 7 | 3:12 | 3:17 | 3:25 |
| VEN. | SAT. | SUN | MOON | MARS | MER. | JUP. | 3:59 | 4: 2 | 4: 6 | 4:10 | 4:15 | 4:21 | 4:28 | 4:38 |
| MER. | JUP. | VEN. | SAT. | SUN | MOON | MARS | 5: 2 | 5: 6 | 5:11 | 5:17 | 5:23 | 5:30 | 5:40 | 5:52 |

# NOVEMBER 1 TO 15, ANY YEAR

## DAY HOURS: SUNRISE TO SUNSET (LOCAL MEAN TIME)

| SUN. | MON. | TU. | WED. | TH. | FRI. | SAT. | LAT. 25° | LAT. 30° | LAT. 35° | LAT. 40° | LAT. 45° | LAT. 50° | LAT. 55° | LAT. 60° |
|---|---|---|---|---|---|---|---|---|---|---|---|---|---|---|
| SUN | MOON | MARS | MER. | JUP. | VEN. | SAT. | 6:15 | 6:23 | 6:32 | 6:41 | 6:53 | 7: 6 | 7:24 | 7:47 |
| VEN. | SAT. | SUN | MOON | MARS | MER. | JUP. | 7:10 | 7:17 | 7:24 | 7:32 | 7:41 | 7:53 | 8: 7 | 8:27 |
| MER. | JUP. | VEN. | SAT. | SUN | MOON | MARS | 8: 5 | 8:10 | 8:16 | 8:22 | 8:30 | 8:39 | 8:50 | 9: 6 |
| MOON | MARS | MER. | JUP. | VEN. | SAT. | SUN | 9: 0 | 9: 3 | 9: 8 | 9:12 | 9:18 | 9:25 | 9:34 | 9:45 |
| SAT. | SUN | MOON | MARS | MER. | JUP. | VEN. | 9:54 | 9:57 | 10: 0 | 10: 3 | 10: 7 | 10:11 | 10:17 | 10:25 |
| JUP. | VEN. | SAT. | SUN | MOON | MARS | MER. | 10:49 | 10:50 | 10:52 | 10:53 | 10:55 | 10:57 | 11: 0 | 11: 4 |
| MARS | MER. | JUP. | VEN. | SAT. | SUN | MOON | 11:44 | 11:44 | 11:44 | 11:44 | 11:44 | 11:43 | 11:43 | 11:43 |
| SUN | MOON | MARS | MER. | JUP. | VEN. | SAT. | 12:38 | 12:37 | 12:36 | 12:34 | 12:32 | 12:30 | 12:27 | 12:23 |
| VEN. | SAT. | SUN | MOON | MARS | MER. | JUP. | 1:33 | 1:30 | 1:28 | 1:24 | 1:20 | 1:16 | 1:10 | 1: 2 |
| MER. | JUP. | VEN. | SAT. | SUN | MOON | MARS | 2:28 | 2:24 | 2:20 | 2:15 | 2: 9 | 2: 2 | 1:53 | 1:41 |
| MOON | MARS | MER. | JUP. | VEN. | SAT. | SUN | 3:22 | 3:17 | 3:12 | 3: 5 | 2:57 | 2:48 | 2:37 | 2:21 |
| SAT. | SUN | MOON | MARS | MER. | JUP. | VEN. | 4:17 | 4:11 | 4: 4 | 3:55 | 3:46 | 3:34 | 3:20 | 3: 0 |

## NIGHT HOURS: SUNSET TO SUNRISE (LOCAL MEAN TIME)

| SUN. | MON. | TU. | WED. | TH. | FRI. | SAT. | LAT. 25° | LAT. 30° | LAT. 35° | LAT. 40° | LAT. 45° | LAT. 50° | LAT. 55° | LAT. 60° |
|---|---|---|---|---|---|---|---|---|---|---|---|---|---|---|
| JUP. | VEN. | SAT. | SUN | MOON | MARS | MER. | 5:12 | 5: 4 | 4:56 | 4:46 | 4:34 | 4:21 | 4: 3 | 3:40 |
| MARS | MER. | JUP. | VEN. | SAT. | SUN | MOON | 6:17 | 6:11 | 6: 4 | 5:55 | 5:46 | 5:34 | 5:20 | 5: 0 |
| SUN | MOON | MARS | MER. | JUP. | VEN. | SAT. | 7:22 | 7:17 | 7:12 | 7: 5 | 6:57 | 6:48 | 6:37 | 6:21 |
| VEN. | SAT. | SUN | MOON | MARS | MER. | JUP. | 8:28 | 8:24 | 8:20 | 8:15 | 8: 9 | 8: 2 | 7:53 | 7:41 |
| MER. | JUP. | VEN. | SAT. | SUN | MOON | MARS | 9:33 | 9:30 | 9:28 | 9:24 | 9:20 | 9:16 | 9:10 | 9: 2 |
| MOON | MARS | MER. | JUP. | VEN. | SAT. | SUN | 10:38 | 10:37 | 10:36 | 10:34 | 10:32 | 10:30 | 10:27 | 10:23 |
| SAT. | SUN | MOON | MARS | MER. | JUP. | VEN. | 11:44 | 11:44 | 11:44 | 11:44 | 11:44 | 11:43 | 11:43 | 11:43 |
| JUP. | VEN. | SAT. | SUN | MOON | MARS | MER. | 12:49 | 12:50 | 12:52 | 12:53 | 12:55 | 12:57 | 1: 0 | 1: 4 |
| MARS | MER. | JUP. | VEN. | SAT. | SUN | MOON | 1:54 | 1:57 | 2: 0 | 2: 3 | 2: 7 | 2:11 | 2:17 | 2:25 |
| SUN | MOON | MARS | MER. | JUP. | VEN. | SAT. | 3: 0 | 3: 3 | 3: 8 | 3:12 | 3:18 | 3:25 | 3:34 | 3:45 |
| VEN. | SAT. | SUN | MOON | MARS | MER. | JUP. | 4: 5 | 4:10 | 4:16 | 4:22 | 4:30 | 4:39 | 4:50 | 5: 6 |
| MER. | JUP. | VEN. | SAT. | SUN | MOON | MARS | 5:10 | 5:17 | 5:24 | 5:32 | 5:41 | 5:53 | 6: 7 | 6:27 |

## DAY HOURS: SUNRISE TO SUNSET (LOCAL MEAN TIME)

| SUN. | MON. | TU. | WED. | TH. | FRI. | SAT. | LAT. 25° | LAT. 30° | LAT. 35° | LAT. 40° | LAT. 45° | LAT. 50° | LAT. 55° | LAT. 60° |
|---|---|---|---|---|---|---|---|---|---|---|---|---|---|---|
| SUN | MOON | MARS | MER. | JUP. | VEN. | SAT. | 6:26 | 6:36 | 6:46 | 6:59 | 7:13 | 7:31 | 7:54 | 8:26 |
| VEN. | SAT. | SUN | MOON | MARS | MER. | JUP. | 7:19 | 7:27 | 7:36 | 7:47 | 7:59 | 8:13 | 8:33 | 8:59 |
| MER. | JUP. | VEN. | SAT. | SUN | MOON | MARS | 8:13 | 8:19 | 8:26 | 8:34 | 8:44 | 8:56 | 9:11 | 9:32 |
| MOON | MARS | MER. | JUP. | VEN. | SAT. | SUN | 9: 6 | 9:11 | 9:16 | 9:22 | 9:30 | 9:39 | 9:50 | 10: 6 |
| SAT. | SUN | MOON | MARS | MER. | JUP. | VEN. | 10: 0 | 10: 3 | 10: 6 | 10:10 | 10:15 | 10:21 | 10:29 | 10:39 |
| JUP. | VEN. | SAT. | SUN | MOON | MARS | MER. | 10:53 | 10:54 | 10:56 | 10:58 | 11: 1 | 11: 4 | 11: 7 | 11:13 |
| MARS | MER. | JUP. | VEN. | SAT. | SUN | MOON | 11:46 | 11:46 | 11:46 | 11:46 | 11:46 | 11:46 | 11:46 | 11:46 |
| SUN | MOON | MARS | MER. | JUP. | VEN. | SAT. | 12:40 | 12:38 | 12:36 | 12:34 | 12:32 | 12:29 | 12:25 | 12:19 |
| VEN. | SAT. | SUN | MOON | MARS | MER. | JUP. | 1:33 | 1:30 | 1:26 | 1:22 | 1:17 | 1:11 | 1: 4 | 12:53 |
| MER. | JUP. | VEN. | SAT. | SUN | MOON | MARS | 2:26 | 2:22 | 2:16 | 2:10 | 2: 3 | 1:54 | 1:42 | 1:26 |
| MOON | MARS | MER. | JUP. | VEN. | SAT. | SUN | 3:20 | 3:13 | 3: 6 | 2:58 | 2:48 | 2:36 | 2:21 | 2: 0 |
| SAT. | SUN | MOON | MARS | MER. | JUP. | VEN. | 4:13 | 4: 5 | 3:56 | 3:46 | 3:34 | 3:19 | 3: 0 | 2:33 |

## NIGHT HOURS: SUNSET TO SUNRISE (LOCAL MEAN TIME)

| SUN. | MON. | TU. | WED. | TH. | FRI. | SAT. | LAT. 25° | LAT. 30° | LAT. 35° | LAT. 40° | LAT. 45° | LAT. 50° | LAT. 55° | LAT. 60° |
|---|---|---|---|---|---|---|---|---|---|---|---|---|---|---|
| JUP. | VEN. | SAT. | SUN | MOON | MARS | MER. | 5: 7 | 4:57 | 4:46 | 4:34 | 4:19 | 4: 1 | 3:38 | 3: 7 |
| MARS | MER. | JUP. | MOON | SAT. | SUN | MOON | 6:13 | 6: 5 | 5:56 | 5:46 | 5:34 | 5:19 | 5: 0 | 4:33 |
| SUN | MOON | MARS | MARS | JUP. | VEN. | SAT. | 7:20 | 7:13 | 7: 6 | 6:58 | 6:48 | 6:36 | 6:21 | 6: 0 |
| VEN. | SAT. | SUN | MER. | MARS | MER. | JUP. | 8:26 | 8:22 | 8:16 | 8:10 | 8: 3 | 7:54 | 7:42 | 7:26 |
| MER. | JUP. | VEN. | JUP. | SUN | MOON | MARS | 9:33 | 9:30 | 9:26 | 9:22 | 9:17 | 9:11 | 9: 4 | 8:53 |
| MOON | MARS | MER. | VEN. | VEN. | SAT. | SUN | 10:40 | 10:38 | 10:36 | 10:34 | 10:32 | 10:29 | 10:25 | 10:19 |
| SAT. | SUN | MOON | SAT. | MER. | JUP. | VEN. | 11:46 | 11:46 | 11:46 | 11:46 | 11:46 | 11:46 | 11:46 | 11:46 |
| JUP. | VEN. | SAT. | SUN | MOON | MARS | MER. | 12:53 | 12:54 | 12:56 | 12:58 | 1: 1 | 1: 4 | 1: 7 | 1:13 |
| MARS | MER. | JUP. | MOON | SAT. | SUN | MOON | 2: 0 | 2: 3 | 2: 6 | 2:10 | 2:15 | 2:21 | 2:29 | 2:39 |
| SUN | MOON | MARS | MARS | JUP. | VEN. | SAT. | 3: 6 | 3:11 | 3:16 | 3:22 | 3:30 | 3:39 | 3:50 | 4: 6 |
| VEN. | SAT. | SUN | MER. | MARS | MER. | JUP. | 4:13 | 4:19 | 4:26 | 4:34 | 4:44 | 4:56 | 5:11 | 5:32 |
| MER. | JUP. | VEN. | JUP. | SUN | MOON | MARS | 5:19 | 5:27 | 5:36 | 5:47 | 5:59 | 6:13 | 6:33 | 6:59 |

# DECEMBER 1 TO 15, ANY YEAR

## DAY HOURS: SUNRISE TO SUNSET (LOCAL MEAN TIME)

| SUN. | MON. | TU. | WED. | TH. | FRI. | SAT. | LAT. 25° | LAT. 30° | LAT. 35° | LAT. 40° | LAT. 45° | LAT. 50° | LAT. 55° | LAT. 60° |
|---|---|---|---|---|---|---|---|---|---|---|---|---|---|---|
| SUN | MOON | MARS | MER. | JUP. | VEN. | SAT. | 6:37 | 6:48 | 7: 0 | 7:14 | 7:31 | 7:51 | 8:18 | 8:57 |
| VEN. | SAT. | SUN | MOON | MARS | MER. | JUP. | 7:29 | 7:38 | 7:48 | 8: 0 | 8:14 | 8:31 | 8:54 | 9:26 |
| MER. | JUP. | VEN. | SAT. | SUN | MOON | MARS | 8:22 | 8:29 | 8:37 | 8:47 | 8:58 | 9:11 | 9:30 | 9:56 |
| MOON | MARS | MER. | JUP. | VEN. | SAT. | SUN | 9:14 | 9:20 | 9:26 | 9:33 | 9:41 | 9:52 | 10: 5 | 10:25 |
| SAT. | SUN | MOON | MARS | MER. | JUP. | VEN. | 10: 7 | 10:10 | 10:14 | 10:19 | 10:25 | 10:32 | 10:41 | 10:54 |
| JUP. | VEN. | SAT. | SUN | MOON | MARS | MER. | 10:59 | 11: 1 | 11: 3 | 11: 5 | 11: 8 | 11:12 | 11:16 | 11:23 |
| MARS | MER. | JUP. | VEN. | SAT. | SUN | MOON | 11:52 | 11:52 | 11:52 | 11:52 | 11:52 | 11:52 | 11:52 | 11:52 |
| SUN | MOON | MARS | MER. | JUP. | VEN. | SAT. | 12:44 | 12:42 | 12:40 | 12:38 | 12:35 | 12:32 | 12:27 | 12:21 |
| VEN. | SAT. | SUN | MOON | MARS | MER. | JUP. | 1:37 | 1:33 | 1:29 | 1:24 | 1:19 | 1:12 | 1: 3 | 12:50 |
| MER. | JUP. | VEN. | SAT. | SUN | MOON | MARS | 2:29 | 2:24 | 2:18 | 2:11 | 2: 2 | 1:52 | 1:38 | 1:19 |
| MOON | MARS | MER. | JUP. | VEN. | SAT. | SUN | 3:22 | 3:15 | 3: 6 | 2:57 | 2:46 | 2:32 | 2:14 | 1:48 |
| SAT. | SUN | MOON | MARS | MER. | JUP. | VEN. | 4:14 | 4: 5 | 3:55 | 3:43 | 3:29 | 3:12 | 2:49 | 2:17 |

## NIGHT HOURS: SUNSET TO SUNRISE (LOCAL MEAN TIME)

| SUN. | MON. | TU. | WED. | TH. | FRI. | SAT. | LAT. 25° | LAT. 30° | LAT. 35° | LAT. 40° | LAT. 45° | LAT. 50° | LAT. 55° | LAT. 60° |
|---|---|---|---|---|---|---|---|---|---|---|---|---|---|---|
| JUP. | VEN. | SAT. | SUN | MOON | MARS | MER. | 5: 7 | 4:56 | 4:44 | 4:30 | 4:13 | 3:52 | 3:25 | 2:46 |
| MARS | MER. | JUP. | VEN. | SAT. | SUN | MOON | 6:14 | 6: 5 | 5:55 | 5:43 | 5:29 | 5:12 | 4:49 | 4:17 |
| SUN | MOON | MARS | MER. | JUP. | VEN. | SAT. | 7:22 | 7:15 | 7: 6 | 6:57 | 6:46 | 6:32 | 6:14 | 5:48 |
| VEN. | SAT. | SUN | MOON | MARS | MER. | JUP. | 8:29 | 8:24 | 8:18 | 8:11 | 8: 2 | 7:52 | 7:38 | 7:19 |
| MER. | JUP. | VEN. | SAT. | SUN | MOON | MARS | 9:37 | 9:33 | 9:29 | 9:24 | 9:19 | 9:12 | 9: 3 | 8:50 |
| MOON | MARS | MER. | JUP. | VEN. | SAT. | SUN | 10:44 | 10:42 | 10:40 | 10:38 | 10:35 | 10:32 | 10:27 | 10:21 |
| SAT. | SUN | MOON | MARS | MER. | JUP. | VEN. | 11:52 | 11:52 | 11:52 | 11:52 | 11:52 | 11:52 | 11:52 | 11:52 |
| JUP. | VEN. | SAT. | SUN | MOON | MARS | MER. | 12:59 | 1: 1 | 1: 3 | 1: 5 | 1: 8 | 1:12 | 1:16 | 1:23 |
| MARS | MER. | JUP. | VEN. | SAT. | SUN | MOON | 2: 7 | 2:10 | 2:14 | 2:19 | 2:25 | 2:32 | 2:41 | 2:54 |
| SUN | MOON | MARS | MER. | JUP. | VEN. | SAT. | 3:14 | 3:20 | 3:26 | 3:33 | 3:41 | 3:52 | 4: 5 | 4:25 |
| VEN. | SAT. | SUN | MOON | MARS | MER. | JUP. | 4:22 | 4:29 | 4:37 | 4:47 | 4:58 | 5:11 | 5:30 | 5:56 |
| MER. | JUP. | VEN. | SAT. | SUN | MOON | MARS | 5:29 | 5:38 | 5:48 | 6: 0 | 6:14 | 6:31 | 6:54 | 7:26 |

# DECEMBER 16 TO 31, ANY YEAR

## DAY HOURS: SUNRISE TO SUNSET (LOCAL MEAN TIME)

| SUN. | MON. | TU. | WED. | TH. | FRI. | SAT. | LAT. 25° | LAT. 30° | LAT. 35° | LAT. 40° | LAT. 45° | LAT. 50° | LAT. 55° | LAT. 60° |
|---|---|---|---|---|---|---|---|---|---|---|---|---|---|---|
| SUN. | MOON | MARS | MER. | JUP. | VEN. | SAT. | 6:46 | 6:57 | 7:10 | 7:25 | 7:42 | 8: 4 | 8:32 | 9:14 |
| VEN. | SAT. | SUN | MOON | MARS | MER. | JUP. | 7:38 | 7:48 | 7:58 | 8:10 | 8:25 | 8:43 | 9: 7 | 9:42 |
| MER. | JUP. | VEN. | SAT. | SUN | MOON | MARS | 8:31 | 8:38 | 8:47 | 8:56 | 9: 8 | 9:22 | 9:41 | 10: 9 |
| MOON | MARS | MER. | JUP. | VEN. | SAT. | SUN | 9:23 | 9:28 | 9:35 | 9:42 | 9:51 | 10: 2 | 10:16 | 10:37 |
| SAT. | SUN | MOON | MARS | MER. | JUP. | VEN. | 10:15 | 10:19 | 10:23 | 10:28 | 10:34 | 10:41 | 10:50 | 11: 4 |
| JUP. | VEN. | SAT. | SUN | MOON | MARS | MER. | 11: 7 | 11: 9 | 11:11 | 11:14 | 11:17 | 11:20 | 11:25 | 11:32 |
| MARS | MER. | JUP. | VEN. | SAT. | SUN | MOON | 12: 0 | 12: 0 | 12: 0 | 12: 0 | 12: 0 | 12: 0 | 12: 0 | 12: 0 |
| SUN | MOON | MARS | MER. | JUP. | VEN. | SAT. | 12:52 | 12:50 | 12:48 | 12:45 | 12:42 | 12:39 | 12:34 | 12:27 |
| VEN. | SAT. | SUN | MOON | MARS | MER. | JUP. | 1:44 | 1:40 | 1:36 | 1:31 | 1:25 | 1:18 | 1: 9 | 12:55 |
| MER. | JUP. | VEN. | SAT. | SUN | MOON | MARS | 2:36 | 2:31 | 2:24 | 2:17 | 2: 8 | 1:57 | 1:43 | 1:22 |
| MOON | MARS | MER. | JUP. | VEN. | SAT. | SUN | 3:29 | 3:21 | 3:13 | 3: 3 | 2:51 | 2:37 | 2:18 | 1:50 |
| SAT. | SUN | MOON | MARS | MER. | JUP. | VEN. | 4:21 | 4:11 | 4: 1 | 3:49 | 3:34 | 3:16 | 2:52 | 2:18 |

## NIGHT HOURS: SUNSET TO SUNRISE (LOCAL MEAN TIME)

| SUN. | MON. | TU. | WED. | TH. | FRI. | SAT. | LAT. 25° | LAT. 30° | LAT. 35° | LAT. 40° | LAT. 45° | LAT. 50° | LAT. 55° | LAT. 60° |
|---|---|---|---|---|---|---|---|---|---|---|---|---|---|---|
| JUP. | VEN. | SAT. | SUN | MOON | MARS | MER. | 5:13 | 5: 2 | 4:49 | 4:34 | 4:17 | 3:55 | 3:27 | 2:45 |
| MARS | MER. | JUP. | VEN. | SAT. | SUN | MOON | 6:21 | 6:11 | 6: 1 | 5:49 | 5:34 | 5:16 | 4:52 | 4:18 |
| SUN | MOON | MARS | MER. | JUP. | VEN. | SAT. | 7:29 | 7:21 | 7:13 | 7: 3 | 6:51 | 6:37 | 6:18 | 5:50 |
| VEN. | SAT. | SUN | MOON | MARS | MER. | JUP. | 8:36 | 8:31 | 8:24 | 8:17 | 8: 8 | 7:57 | 7:43 | 7:22 |
| MER. | JUP. | VEN. | SAT. | SUN | MOON | MARS | 9:44 | 9:40 | 9:36 | 9:31 | 9:25 | 9:18 | 9: 9 | 8:55 |
| MOON | MARS | MER. | JUP. | VEN. | SAT. | SUN | 10:52 | 10:50 | 10:48 | 10:45 | 10:42 | 10:39 | 10:34 | 10:27 |
| SAT. | SUN | MOON | MARS | MER. | JUP. | VEN. | 12: 2 | 12: 2 | 12: 2 | 12: 2 | 12: 2 | 12: 2 | 12: 2 | 12: 2 |
| JUP. | VEN. | SAT. | SUN | MOON | MARS | MER. | 1: 7 | 1: 9 | 1:11 | 1:14 | 1:17 | 1:20 | 1:25 | 1:32 |
| MARS | MER. | JUP. | VEN. | SAT. | SUN | MOON | 2:15 | 2:19 | 2:23 | 2:28 | 2:34 | 2:41 | 2:50 | 3: 4 |
| SUN | MOON | MARS | MER. | JUP. | VEN. | SAT. | 3:23 | 3:28 | 3:35 | 3:42 | 3:51 | 4: 2 | 4:16 | 4:37 |
| VEN. | SAT. | SUN | MOON | MARS | MER. | JUP. | 4:31 | 4:38 | 4:47 | 4:56 | 5: 8 | 5:22 | 5:41 | 6: 9 |
| MER. | JUP. | VEN. | SAT. | SUN | MOON | MARS | 5:38 | 5:48 | 5:58 | 6:10 | 6:25 | 6:43 | 7: 7 | 7:42 |

## THE EVERYDAY RHYTHM OF LIFE

SATURN'S HOUR IDENTIFIES A MOMENTARY PHASE OF REALITY in which an emphasis of remote relevancies can become quite important. A particular development of seminal ideas may challenge prevailing assumption. There can always be some assurance of immortality or encouragement for long-range achievement. Here SENSITIVENESS, at best, can strengthen man's overall breadth of realization, but, at worst, feed his undisciplined delusions. This hour can be chosen for action or consideration in order to advance definite ultimacies or it can be found to reveal overall deficiency that must be overcome.

JUPITER'S HOUR IDENTIFIES A MOMENTARY PHASE OF REALITY in which an emphasis of broad, or overall self-realization can challenge unrealized personal capacities. What can come forward might tend to expand and unfetter selfhood in one way or another, or somehow encourage all effort toward individual distinction. Here ENTHUSIASM, at best, can enhance a very effective self-expression but, at worst, encourage unbridled dissipation. This hour can be chosen for action or consideration in order to advance high personal self-realization, or it can reveal elements of prodigality or sheer recklessness that need to be checked.

MARS' HOUR IDENTIFIES A MOMENTARY PHASE OF REALITY in which there is likely an emphasis of the individual's effort to get established in a basic culture, or a business, or a religious body, or other interweaving group relationship, and so an aggressive tendency of some sort. The capacity to start things that frame and refine selfhood, in its more practical identity, can be helped to precipitate trouble or break through barriers. What is stimulated in this hour is fundamentally a simple aliveness, and it is the foundation of the efficiency that man must possess to some extent but that often falls short into fruitless incompetence. Here, INITIATIVE can ceaselessly make do with illimitable variety of elements in the universal flux of things, but, at worst, it contributes to waste and destructive confusion. This hour can be chosen for action or consideration in order to ad-

vance specific progress of any sort, or it can reveal dangerous inadequacy.

THE SUN'S HOUR IDENTIFIES A MOMENTARY PHASE OF REALITY
in which there is emphasis on the endless necessity of the
human creature to mediate at all points of eventuation
between the deeper, or enduring, or perhaps spiritual,
makeup of itself on the one side and its transient, or ever-
shifting and practical, or convenient self-manifestation as
the essentially physical individual on the other. This eternal
mediator is essentially the simple ego that can represent
divinity and depravity in the everyday partnerships of experience, and so be god or devil with equal facility. Here
PURPOSE best stabilizes integrity and gives dignity to decision, but, at worst, instruments the psychologically suicidal
surrender of man to the complete disintegration of his
character. This hour can be chosen for action or consideration in order to advance illimitable personal accomplishment, or it can reveal the disordered egotism leading
to many ills until its course is stopped.

THE VENUS HOUR IDENTIFIES A MOMENTARY PHASE OF REAL-
ITY in which there is emphasis of the common effort of man
to maneuver the tangible properties of interweaving group
relationships for individual advantage, or perhaps of the
special necessity for a possessive concern over things as
symbols of reliably enduring value. This capacity to complete, or round out, or cherish the everyday objects of
commonplace realities, is fundamentally esthetic appreciation and often of very happy presence. It is the ultimate
manifestation of the social or communal efficiency that
men almost universally strive to achieve through the exercise and preservation of their distinctive cultural patterns.
Here ACQUISITIVENESS, at best, shows man as he tirelessly
courts both the resources and beauties of life, but, at worst,
as he betrays his birthright by unbridled selfishness. This
hour can be chosen for action or consideration in order to
advance the continual enhancement of human existence, or
it can reveal sheer debasement of living.

MERCURY'S HOUR IDENTIFIES A MOMENTARY PHASE OF REAL-
ITY in which an emphasis of the commonplace affairs of
interweaving group relationships in any sort of human
existence can become very significant in essentially imaginative or completely symbolized detail, or in which every
possible sort of reality may be manipulated by representation as thereupon a contribution to perspective, or a
challenge to understanding. This capacity to think in an-
ticipation of act, in every possible sense, is the intellectual
efficiency that distinguishes man from the other animals.
Here MENTALITY, at best, frees the individual from all bond-
age to life's material objectivity, but, at worst, plunges him
into every possible illusory aspect of reality. This hour can
be chosen for action or consideration in order to advance
full realization of any desired sort, or it can reveal mental
inadequacy that needs serious attention.

THE MOON'S HOUR IDENTIFIES A MOMENTARY PHASE OF REAL-
ITY in which there is an emphasis of the endless necessity to
adjust at all points of eventuation between the collective
whole of individual makeup and the complementary total
of all other human manifestation. This is public awareness
and conscious realization of environment, or what constitutes the civilized man, and the lesser light defines the
challenge and achievements in the course of all this either in
the background, or coming to significant manifestation.
Here FEELING, at best, enriches any or all activity and concern of this sort, but, at worst, reveals its needless degenera-
tion into prejudice or bigotry and destructive divisiveness.
This hour can be chosen for action or consideration in
order to advance the everyday place of the self in life at
large, or it can reveal general dissociation from the whole
real scheme of existence.

# PART II

## *PERSONAL ASTROLOGY BY USE OF AN EPHEMERIS*

## Chapter Four

# CYCLES OF IMMEDIACY

With the swifter moving planets it is necessary to know their zodiacal positions more precisely than has been the case with the outermost and slower ones, and now, in consequence, to possess or have access to one of the widely available tabulations of these positions. They are found in an astrological ephemeris. Unhappily, this is quite different for every year. That becomes a problem for anyone going at all deeply into astrology, and so encountering birth times ranging over as much as a century. In the present pages the need of the moment is for the current year only. Moreover, the newcomer in this fascinating field of interest would be very wise to avoid concerning himself with the total and large spread of information in these ephemerides. Instead, he should restrict his attention to the planetary places for which he now has use. These are given in celestial longitude (abbreviated as long.) by degrees and minutes of zodiacal sign as, say Aries 19°19′ for Jupiter at the chance moment this line is being written.

Customarily the symbols for degrees (°) and minute (′) appear at the top of the column, and the symbol of the sign is placed between the degrees and minutes thus 19° ♈ 19′. Also in the same position may appear an "R" in the line for the day of the month in which the given planet is stationary in turning to retrograde motion, and a "D" similarly when it turns back to its direct and usual course. Instead of the simple "R" the astrologers have made wise use of the letter with a stroke (thus ℞) which is the physician's symbol for a prescription (recipe in Latin). It is important to remember that the longitude here, showing zodiacal place in the heavens, is quite different from the terrestrial longitude used to mark the geographical place by meridian of a location somewhere around the earth. The term latitude also refers to two different measures, and it has been encountered in its geographical form in determining the planetary hours. Its celestial or astronomical form has no present astrological importance.

When it came to the current positions by zodiacal sign of Jupiter, Mars, the sun, Venus, Mercury and the moon, the spans marked out in time are too short to make it practical to tabulate the likely nature of a quarter century of these in round terms. That has been practical only with the four planets Pluto through Saturn. It has been possible, however, to include the sun more thoroughly and the moon quite preliminary in Part One by some variation of approach. At this point the current ephemeris is needed for very specialized astrology. Of course, it now will be possible for the earlier procedures to be made more precise in any particular instance. But any more specific dating would not eliminate the tendency of these longer periods, embracing all people everywhere, to overlap each other to some appreciable extent.

The overlapping must not be visualized as any modification of something by something else relevant to it. Rather what will be observed is the persistence, for a little while, of elements of preceding nature as those of the succeeding sort begin to give the evidence of themselves. In a proper astrology there is never an actual mix of indications, but always continuance of transition from a former to a later state of being. Here, in the most simple of terms, is growth. Adulthood is no less essentially what it is even when a surviving adolescence, may crop out momentarily and be just as certainly what it always has been. Beginnings and endings are almost inevitably staggered in all human experience. It only adds up to mental confusion when the meaning of the sign Taurus, for example, is thought to be less itself and more an amalgam of Aries at its cusp or threshold, or conversely when Aries is believed to be thinned out by the essence of Taurus as it approaches the same boundary on the other side.

The phenomenon of sequence is quite different from an infinite regression which is in modification of everything by everything else, in one fashion or another. It is blending of all things into utterly fluid service to all other thing. This is illustrated most fundamentally in the horoscopic elements, taken in ever-varying successive relationships with each other. This characterizes the zodiacal signs — Aries through Pisces — and the specific order of the original seven planets, Saturn through the moon, and around endlessly. In growth as well as in any form of functional organization there are always adjacencies as the core pattern of a momentary reality. Any understanding of this can lead to high skill in putting matters of concern in line, or eliminating what is of no importance and embracing what can be truly crucial in self-interest.

## BASIC PERSONALITY

JUPITER WHILE MOVING THROUGH ARIES reveals a general trend toward ASPIRATION in human makeup. This, while capitalizing on a preceding special stimulus of SYMPATHY, begins to build toward a heightened realization of the personality's fundamental VIRILITY. Life is enhanced as there is reasonable response to these psychological tides. If the prior approximate year has been characterized by any drawing of self out of itself in association with others, it is possible in this following period to inaugurate significant personal redirection.

JUPITER WHILE MOVING THROUGH TAURUS reveals a general trend toward VIRILITY in human makeup. This, while capitalizing on a preceding special stimulus of ASPIRATION, begins to build toward a heightened realization of the personality's VIVIFICATION. Life is enhanced as there is reasonable response to these psychological tides. If the prior approximate year has been characterized by any exceptional or ambitious outreach of the self, it is possible in this following period to bring almost any matter of concern to very effective and practical operation.

JUPITER WHILE MOVING THROUGH GEMINI reveals a general trend toward VIVIFICATION in human makeup. This, while capitalizing on a preceding special stimulus of VIRILITY, begins to build toward a heightened realization of the personality's fundamental EXPANSION. Life is enhanced as there is reasonable response to these psychological tides. If the prior approximate year has been characterized by any successful manifestation of the sheer power of presence by the self, it is possible in this following period to launch some sort of practical enterprise and to endow it with enduring potential.

JUPITER WHILE MOVING THROUGH CANCER reveals a general trend toward EXPANSION in human makeup. This, while capitalizing on a preceding special stimulus of VIVIFICATION, begins to build toward a heightened realization of the personality's fundamental ASSURANCE. Life is enhanced as there is reasonable response to these psychological tides. If the prior approximate year has been characterized by any particular achievement in launching or promoting significant activities of some sort, it is possible in this following period to broaden the activity or widen the scope in quite dramatic fashion of whatever may come to attention or concern.

JUPITER WHILE MOVING THROUGH LEO reveals a general trend toward ASSURANCE in human makeup. This, while capitalizing on a preceding special stimulus of EXPANSION, begins to build toward a heightened realization of the personality's fundamental ASSIMILATION. Life is enhanced as there is reasonable response to these psychological tides. If the prior approximate year has been characterized by any appreciable broadening of activities and responsibilities, it is possible in this following period to grasp perhaps illimitable opportunities and bring them under firm control.

JUPITER WHILE MOVING THROUGH VIRGO reveals a general trend toward ASSIMILATION in human makeup. This, while capitalizing on a preceding special stimulus of ASSURANCE, begins to build toward a heightened realization of the personality's fundamental EQUIVALENCE. Life is enhanced as there is reasonable response to these psychological tides. If the prior approximate year has been characterized by a real demonstration of a power to bring things to disciplined order and hold them there, it is possible in this following period to handle all the current vicissitudes of everyday affairs with exceptional resourcefulness.

JUPITER WHILE MOVING THROUGH LIBRA reveals a general trend toward EQUIVALENCE in human makeup. This, while capitalizing on a preceding special stimulus of ASSIMILATION, begins to build toward a heightened realization of the personality's fundamental CREATIVITY. Life is enhanced as there is reasonable response to these psychological tides. If the prior approximate year has been characterized by the manifestation of some particularly unusual gift for dealing with the confusions of daily living, it is possible in this following period to bring perhaps very brilliant reconciliations about and thus contribute to current progress.

JUPITER WHILE MOVING THROUGH SCORPIO reveals a general trend toward CREATIVITY in human makeup. This, while capitalizing on a preceding special stimulus of EQUIVALENCE, begins to build toward a heightened realization of the personality's fundamental ADMINISTRATION. Life is enhanced as there is reasonable response to these psychological tides. If the prior approximate year has been characterized by perhaps very dramatic personal realignments leading to significant progress, it is possible in this following period to give full and successful rein to almost any sort of unique or pet project of self-expression.

JUPITER WHILE MOVING THROUGH SAGITTARIUS reveals a general trend toward ADMINISTRATION in human makeup. This, while capitalizing on a preceding special stimulus of CREATIVITY, begins to build toward a heightened realization of the personality's fundamental DISCRIMINATION. Life is enhanced as there is a reasonable response to these psychological tides. If the prior approximate year has been characterized by some strikingly original approach to previously unsolved problems, it is possible in this following period to take very successful steps forward in dealing with any confusions of the moment.

JUPITER WHILE MOVING THROUGH CAPRICORN reveals a general trend toward DISCRIMINATION in human makeup. This, while capitalizing on a preceding special stimulus of

ADMINISTRATION, begins to build toward a heightened realization of the personality's fundamental LOYALTY. Life is
enhanced as there is reasonable response to these psychological tides. If the prior approximate year has been characterized by exceptionally uninhibited striding forward to
significant performance step after step, it is possible in this
following period to get almost anything of worth in firm
stabilized form.

JUPITER WHILE MOVING THROUGH AQUARIUS reveals a general trend toward LOYALTY in human makeup. This, while
capitalizing on a preceding special stimulus of DIS-
CRIMINATION, begins to build toward a heightened realization of personality's fundamental SYMPATHY. Life is enhanced as there is reasonable response to these psychological tides. If the prior approximate year has been characterized by some dramatic competence in the practical ordering of things in the face of crisis, it is possible in this
following period to establish support of illimitable spread
and depth for almost any promising enterprise.

JUPITER WHILE MOVING THROUGH PISCES reveals a general
trend toward SYMPATHY in human makeup. This, while
capitalizing on a preceding special stimulus of LOYALTY,
begins to build toward a heightened realization of personality's fundamental ASPIRATION. Life is enhanced as
there is reasonable response to these psychological tides. If
the prior approximate year has been characterized by spectacular rallying to the support and advance of genuinely
worthy projects and agencies, it is possible in this following
period to inaugurate or enlarge any tangible manifestation
of mankind's hope and vision.

## PRACTICAL ACTIVITY

Mars and Venus are much alike in the irregularity of
their retrogradation in the zodiac, as neither (1) syste-
matically once a year as with Jupiter and the others on out,
nor (2) several times annually as with Mercury. In more or
less normal course, or when not too close to retrograding,
Mars moves considerably slower than the sun and Venus

slightly faster. The former is thus a little more like the distant planets, and in consequence its immediacy cycles can be seen to be more primarily or impersonally dynamic.

MARS WHILE MOVING THROUGH ARIES reveals a current emphasis of ASPIRATION as unconditioned elbowroom for accomplishment preliminarily stimulated by self-releasing sympathy and now, at best, to be directed into self-maintained VIRILITY. Life may be found quickened to sudden new interests. If the preceding several weeks have been especially restless for an individual, he may, for this period, know that he stands at some particular threshold of personal opportunity.

MARS WHILE MOVING THROUGH TAURUS reveals a current emphasis of VIRILITY as broadened elbowroom for a thorough self-expenditure preliminarily stimulated by self-stirring ASPIRATION and now, at best, to be directed into significant VIVIFICATION of some practical nature. Life may be found quickened to very pertinent potentialities. If the preceding several weeks have been especially challenging or personally exciting for an individual, he may, for this period, know that he stands at some particular threshold of gratifying self-expenditure.

MARS WHILE MOVING THROUGH GEMINI reveals a current emphasis of VIVIFICATION as highly creative elbowroom for the practical impact of self on other people preliminarily stimulated by its sheer VIRILITY and now, at best, to be directed to significant EXPANSION of all manifestation of selfhood. Life may be found quickened to the simple joy of uninhibited expression of itself. If the preceding several weeks have been especially, but profitably, exacting for an individual, he may, for this period, know that he stands at some particular threshold of vital significance to others around him.

MARS WHILE MOVING THROUGH CANCER reveals a current emphasis of EXPANSION as exceptionally practical elbowroom for an immediately widening reality preliminarily stimulated by a personal VIVIFICATION and now, at best, to be built into a competent and growing ASSURANCE. Life may be found quickened to a new breadth of significance. If the preceding several weeks have been unusually relaxing and happy for an individual, he may, for this period, know that he stands at some particular threshold of far greater and more wide-ranging relations with his fellows.

MARS WHILE MOVING THROUGH LEO reveals a current emphasis of ASSURANCE as exceptionally effective elbowroom for self-identity stimulated by a thoroughgoing and unlimited EXPANSION and now able, at best, to contribute to a genuinely definitive ASSIMILATION. Life may be found quickened to greatly sharpened issues and unusually dramatized concerns. If the preceding several weeks have been especially broadening for an individual's mind and heart he may, for this period, know that he stands at some particular threshold of distinctive self-realization.

MARS WHILE MOVING THROUGH VIRGO reveals a current emphasis of ASSIMILATION as endless elbowroom for bringing into the basic substance of self whatever has been enriched and stimulated by ASSURANCE and now, at best, can help establish a genuine ground for EQUIVALENCE in commonplace relationships. Life may be found quickened to a gratifying effectiveness in human intimacies or productive dependence on each other. If the preceding several weeks have been especially helpful in building up an individual's proper self-confidence he may, for this period, know that he stands at some particular threshold of socioeconomic advancement for himself and those having close ties with him.

MARS WHILE MOVING THROUGH LIBRA reveals a current emphasis of EQUIVALENCE as wide-ranging and intelligent elbowroom for co-operative associations arising from or stimulated by ASSIMILATION and now likely to provide vital and convenient fulfillment of self-potential in an essential CREATIVITY. Life may be found quickened to possibly spectacular realignments in the more important human interrelations. If the preceding several weeks have been especially prodigal in the shuffling of things to the special advantage of an individual he may, for this period, know that he stands at some particular threshold of high personal opportunity in his usual realms of activity.

MARS WHILE MOVING THROUGH SCORPIO reveals a current

emphasis of CREATIVITY as self-established and self-maintained elbowroom for unusually specialized and often exceptionally valuable effort through stimulated EQUIVALENCE or ramifying mutualities of concern and now, at best, able to contribute ultimately to ADMINISTRATION or effective direction in human affairs. Life may be found quickened to very pertinent extemporizations and experimentations. If the preceding several weeks have been especially helpful in reshaping everyday common contacts in significant fashion for an individual he may, for this period, know that he stands at some particular threshold of uninhibited release of unsuspected capacity in his makeup.

MARS WHILE MOVING THROUGH SAGITTARIUS reveals a current emphasis of ADMINISTRATION as the basic socio-economic elbowroom made possible in an industrialized society. It is stimulated through CREATIVITY and now to be brought to effective operation in a modern DISCRIMINATION. Life may be found quickened by the convenience of the illimitable facilities and gadgets of civilization and ramifying detail of their production and distribution. If the preceding several weeks have been especially helpful through any sudden or surprising developments in his personal economy an individual may, for this period, know that he stands at some particular threshold of enlarged self-dimension to which he should give real attention.

MARS WHILE MOVING THROUGH CAPRICORN reveals a current emphasis of DISCRIMINATION as the mental elbowroom required for any effective conscious existence in the complicated modern world. It is ever stimulated by the broadening ADMINISTRATION established and re-established and, now of necessity, directed to the LOYALTY that ultimately and alone can bring a global humanity together and hold them in common pattern. Life may be found to quicken to the increasing necessity of law and cultural mores by which everyday affairs are able to continue in course. If the preceding several weeks have been especially dominated by dramatic leadership in crisis an individual way, for this period, know that he stands at some particular threshold of sound evaluation of which he should take prompt advantage.

MARS WHILE MOVING THROUGH AQUARIUS reveals a current emphasis of LOYALTY as illimitable and essentially emotional elbowroom for facilitating relations with other people and special causes. It is stimulated through DISCRIMINATION and now able, in due course, to contribute to a larger and overall SYMPATHY. Life may be found quickened to unusual effort to develop a more effective rapport in all human affairs. If the preceding several weeks have been especially characteristic by enlightened, and momentarily striking, demonstrations of any bettering practical spirit among his associates an individual may, for this period, know that he stands at some particular threshold of self-alignment with the enduring potentials of mankind.

MARS WHILE MOVING THROUGH PISCES reveals a current emphasis of SYMPATHY as a thoroughly universalized but almost passionate elbowroom. It is stimulated by every well-tested LOYALTY and now, at best, directed to the strengthening of the most fainthearted of man as they seek to express themselves in their ASPIRATION. Life may be found quickened by the instinctive drawing together of men in these times when acting too much alone can be altogether frustrating. If the preceding several weeks have been especially rich in human associations, and there have been repetitive cases of almost dramatic helpfulness in daily ongoing an individual may, for this period, know that he stands at some particular threshold of greater dimension of living.

## SELF-INTEREST

Venus, together with Mercury, (since in symbolical significance their zodiacal cycles are established inside the orbit of the earth) become indicators of man's fundamental intimacies in the overall context of his immediate affairs. The phase of this charted by Venus is his enlistment of the tangible objects of life for his own use, or a bringing of the potentials of the world at large to his individual service. This can be for enjoyment or reward, but it can be also for very practical support or relevant instrumentation. Psychologically it is the necessity for love and appreciation and, on less personal and more impartial levels, the agencies and appurtenances of everyday and ordinary accomplishment.

VENUS WHILE MOVING THROUGH ARIES reveals the effective support of an individual's ASPIRATION as he has been able to cultivate it through a practical SYMPATHY with the everyday world in which he finds himself and as this becomes a challenge to his VIRILITY. Life here is seen likely to provide the assistance necessary for any enduring self-interest. If the preceding months have actually been marked by outstanding personal benefit from passing eventuations, the individual may, for this period, know that he stands at some particular threshold of expanded self-realization.

VENUS WHILE MOVING THROUGH TAURUS reveals the effective support of an individual's VIRILITY as he has been able to cultivate it through a practical ASPIRATION in the everyday world in which he finds himself and as it becomes a challenge to his VIVIFICATION. Life here is seen likely to provide the specific assistance necessary for any enduring self-interest. If the preceding several months have actually been marked by exceptionally significant support for some unusually inspired effort of his, the individual may, for this period, know that he stands at the threshold of perhaps dramatic self-expenditures.

VENUS WHILE MOVING THROUGH GEMINI reveals the effective support of an individual's VIVIFICATION as he has been able to cultivate it through a practical VIRILITY in the everyday world in which he finds himself and as it becomes a challenge to his EXPANSION of his current activities. Life here is seen likely to provide the specific assistance necessary for any enduring self-interests. If the preceding several months have actually been marked by perhaps striking success in rising to important issues and taking thoroughgoing advantage of them, the individual may, for this period, know that he stands at some particular threshold of genuine self-establishment.

VENUS WHILE MOVING THROUGH CANCER reveals the effective support of an individual's EXPANSION of his current affairs as he has been able to cultivate it through a practical

VIVIFICATION or successful restructuring of them in some skillful fashion and as that has become challenge to his fundamental ASSURANCE. Life here is seen likely to provide the specific assistance necessary for any enduring self-interest. If the preceding several months have actually been marked by some striking mobilization of specific skills or capacities, and with special success in using them, the individual may know, for this period, know that he stands at the threshold of some most gratifying enlargement of his overall orientations.

VENUS WHILE MOVING THROUGH LEO reveals the effective support of an individual's ASSURANCE as he has been able to cultivate it through a practical EXPANSION of relative concern and as this has become a challenge to his ASSIMILATION or capacity for bringing the things of real importance into a workable piece. Life here is seen likely to provide the specific assistance necessary for any enduring self-interest. If the preceding several months have been marked by perhaps extraordinary increase of breadth and scope of personal affairs the individual may, for this period, know that he stands at some threshold of very significant recognition.

VENUS WHILE MOVING THROUGH VIRGO reveals the effective support of an individual's ASSIMILATION through special ordering of things for his own convenience as he has been stimulated to this through a definite cultivation of his ASSURANCE and as this has become a challenge to his EQUIVALENCE capacity to bring virtually all things into a proper balance with each other. Life here is seen likely to provide the specific assistance necessary for any enduring self-interest. If the preceding several months have actually been marked by eventuations bringing him forward to, perhaps, very dramatic prominence for the moment the individual may, for this period, know that he stands at some threshold of unusually rewarding self-refinement.

VENUS WHILE MOVING THROUGH LIBRA reveals the effective support of an individual's EQUIVALENCE, or capacity to establish a relevant balance of things, following his cultivation of ASSIMILATION, or ability to bring everything of any relevance into his own patterning, and as this becomes a challenge to his CREATIVITY, through which he transforms them or re-adapts them to greater pertinence. Life here is seen likely to provide the specific assistance necessary for any enduring self-interest. If the preceding several months have been particularly marked by outstanding success in getting general matters of crucial concern into manageable arrangement, the individual may, for this period, know that he stands at some sharp threshold of perhaps revolutionary potentialities.

VENUS WHILE MOVING THROUGH SCORPIO reveals the effective support of an individual's CREATIVITY in the fruitful reshaping of things cultivated by the recognition of all relevant EQUIVALENCE or balancing of pertinent factors and as this becomes a challenge to significant ADMINISTRATION or the proper distribution of the benefits. Life here is seen likely to provide the specific assistance necessary for any enduring self-interest. If the preceding several months have been actually marked by unexpected and striking manipulation of matters of concern in order to bring them together as accomplished, the individual, may for this period, know that he stands at some particular threshold of a newly established opportunity.

VENUS WHILE MOVING THROUGH SAGITTARIUS reveals the effective support of an individual's ADMINISTRATION of his affairs cultivated by relevant CREATIVITY, or reshaping of things to his own ends and as now he builds on toward a significant DISCRIMINATION. Life here is seen likely to provide the specific assistance necessary for any enduring self-interest. If the preceding several months have been marked by dramatically successful resourcefulness at some very critical juncture the individual may, for this period, know that he stands at the threshold of an exceptional challenge to leadership opening up for him.

VENUS WHILE MOVING THROUGH CAPRICORN reveals the effective support of an individual's DISCRIMINATION as this has been cultivated by a relevant ADMINISTRATION and now can contribute vitally to an important LOYALTY or capacity to establish values in proper alignment with definitely broader trends in everyday affairs. Life here is seen likely to provide the specific assistance necessary for any enduring self-interest. If the preceding several months actually have been marked by striking effective manipulation of people and authority in connection with prevailing confusions of any sort, the individual may, for this period, know that he stands at some particular threshold of juristic, or political, or institutional challenge that can bring him real distinction.

VENUS WHILE MOVING THROUGH AQUARIUS reveals the effective support of an individual's LOYALTY, or establishment of definitive alignments in overall acceptance as cultivated by relevant DISCRIMINATION and as this can challenge him toward a truly significant SYMPATHY, or exceptional capacity to throw the whole of himself into every phase of human experience. Life here is seen likely to provide the specific assistance necessary for any enduring self-interest. If the preceding several months have actually been marked by sudden and exceptionally sound and dramatic realization of the greater depths underlying everyday affairs the individual may, for this period, know that he stands at some threshold of opportunity for perhaps a truly enduring self-direction.

VENUS WHILE MOVING THROUGH PISCES reveals the effective support of an individual's SYMPATHY, or self-alignment to the more vital substance of human experience as this has been cultivated by a relevant LOYALTY, or foundational anchorage in established values and concepts and as this can contribute to man's significant ASPIRATION or his bringing of his efforts to single and pertinent point of critical moment. Life here is seen likely always to provide the specific assistance necessary for any enduring self-interest. If the preceding several months have been marked by exceptional dramatization and highly successful exposition of significant standards or special causes of striking scope the individual may, for this period, know that he stands at some particular threshold of truly outstanding self-fulfillment.

## *BASIC INTELLIGENCE*

Astrologers have long considered Mercury to be the most intimate in its indication of all the planets. Closest to the sun by orbit, it has been taken as the special messenger or, in a way, the advance agent of man's will or purpose. In everyday actuality this becomes his MENTALITY, or his capacity in his high stage of evolution to manipulate the representation of things through their symbols. This permits him to try out eventuality before it happens, and, in the tentativeness, choose and select and ultimately control his life to a very great extent. Here is his intelligence or understanding for better or worse.

The many retrogradations of Mercury, occurring for some twenty-three days slightly more than three times a year, help provide an astrological measure for the consistent pro-and-con nature of intellect. When this planet is retrograde, any situation in life may tend to be more gestative than productive. Hence an astrologer, as in the case of the moon while decreasing in light, may suggest an avoidance of positive act or decision. This procedure can be too literal an attempt to live with the stars, as already suggested. When horoscopic indications or actual situations are momentarily more subjective from a normal definitiveness, it is wiser to deal with any issues on a psychological level as far as possible.

MERCURY WHILE MOVING THROUGH ARIES reveals a mental freshness of outlook identified as an ASPIRATION, properly strengthened by a mental breadth of SYMPATHY, and building toward the mental courage of VIRILITY. The mind, of course, must be particularly alert to these rhythmic cycles of human awareness. Thus, in the preceding months if there has been dramatic quickening of self-realization through emotional involvements, an individual may know that he might have a significant development of his ambition along well-established lines.

MERCURY WHILE MOVING THROUGH TAURUS reveals a mental courage of understanding identified as a VIRILITY, properly strengthened by the mental freshness of ASPIRATION, and building toward the mental exuberance of VIVIFICATION. The mind, of course, must be particularly alert to these rhythmic cycles of human awareness. Thus, in the preceding months if there has been dramatic quickening of self-realization through some successful culmination of personal ambition, an individual may know that he might now have special opportunity to uncover or exploit perhaps totally unrealized capacities and assets.

MERCURY WHILE MOVING THROUGH GEMINI reveals a mental exuberance of spirit identified as a VIVIFICATION, properly strengthened by the mental courage of VIRILITY, and building toward the mental comprehensiveness of EXPANSION. The mind, of course, must be particularly alert to these rhythmic cycles of human awareness. Thus, in the preceding months if there has been dramatic quickening of self-realization through some practical utilization or special conservation of personal resources, an individual may know that he might now have an exceptional and gratifying success in the inauguration, or advancement of another highly significant enterprise.

MERCURY WHILE MOVING THROUGH CANCER reveals a mental comprehensiveness of interest identified as an EXPANSION, properly strengthened by the mental exuberance of VIVIFICATION, and building toward singleness in the mental perspective of ASSURANCE. The mind, of course, must be particularly alert to these rhythmic cycles of human awareness. Thus, in the preceding months, if there has been dramatic quickening of self-realization through success in originating or developing some special project or program, an individual may know that he might now have some sort of broadening of the scope in his affairs.

MERCURY WHILE MOVING THROUGH LEO reveals a mental singleness of perspective identified as an ASSURANCE, properly strengthened by the mental comprehensiveness of EXPANSION, and building toward the mental integrity of ASSIMILATION. The mind, of course, must be particularly alert to these rhythmic cycles of human awareness. Thus, in the preceding months, if there has been a dramatic quickening of self-realization through a broadening of personal affairs in perhaps many directions, an individual may know that he might now have some very gratifying recognition, or elevation in dignity.

MERCURY WHILE MOVING THROUGH VIRGO reveals a mental integrity of concern identified as an ASSIMILATION, properly strengthened by the mental singleness of perspective of ASSURANCE, and building toward the mental directness of EQUIVALENCE. The mind, of course, must be particularly alert to these rhythmic cycles of human awareness. Thus, in the preceding months, if there has been a dramatic quickening of self-realization through some very marked achievement in authoritative response to crisis or conflict, an individual may know that he now has some special opportunity for straightening out, or reordering, materials or interconnections of high significance.

MERCURY WHILE MOVING THROUGH LIBRA reveals a mental directness of relationship identified as EQUIVALENCE, properly strengthened by the mental integrity of concern of ASSIMILATION, and so building toward the mental alchemy of CREATIVITY. The mind, of course, must be particularly alert to these rhythmic cycles of human awareness. Thus, in the preceding months, if there has been a dramatic quickening of self-realization through especially efficient troubleshooting of some sort in significant circumstances, an individual may now know that he might have the chance to mediate more spectacular conflict or reconcile almost impossible differences.

MERCURY WHILE MOVING THROUGH SCORPIO reveals a mental alchemy of judgment identified as CREATIVITY, properly strengthened by the mental directness of EQUIVALENCE, and building toward the mental adroitness of ADMINISTRATION. The mind, of course, must be particularly alert to these rhythmic cycles of human awareness. Thus, in the preceding months, if there has been a dramatic quickening of self-realization, through an effective balancing of things at crucial moments, an individual may know that he might be enlisted in extraordinary exacting investigation carrying him to vital significance.

MERCURY MOVING THROUGH SAGITTARIUS reveals a mental

adroitness of decision identified as ADMINISTRATION, properly strengthened by the mental alchemy of CREATIVITY, and building toward the mental ordering of discrimination. The mind, of course, must be particularly alert to these rhythmic cycles of human awareness. Thus, in the preceding months, if there has been dramatic quickening of self-realization through a drastic remolding of functions and conceptions, in some important juncture, an individual may know that he might be given or acquire significant high business or political responsibilities.

MERCURY MOVING THROUGH CAPRICORN reveals a mental ordering of differences identified as DISCRIMINATION, properly strengthened by the adroitness of ADMINISTRATION, and building toward the real depth of LOYALTY. The mind, of course, must be particularly alert to these rhythmic cycles of human awareness. Thus, in the preceding months, if there has been a markedly successful exercise of authority under very special conditions, an individual may not know that he might have the chance for very significant ordering or stabilizing of other current affairs.

MERCURY MOVING THROUGH AQUARIUS reveals a mental depth of relationship identified as LOYALTY, properly strengthened by the mental ordering of DISCRIMINATION, and building toward the mental breadth of SYMPATHY. The mind, of course, must be particularly alert to these rhythmic cycles of human awareness. Thus, in the preceding months, if there has been some marked achievement in the clarification of controversy or validation of vital operations, an individual may now know that he might have unusual opportunity for enlisting his fellows and himself in some unusually worthwhile cause or venture.

MERCURY MOVING THROUGH PISCES reveals a mental breadth of concern identified as SYMPATHY, properly strengthened by the mental depth of LOYALTY, and building toward the mental freshness in outlook of ASPIRATION. The mind, of course, must be particularly alert to these rhythmic cycles of human awareness. Thus, in the preceding months, if there has been a marked development of cohesiveness of idea and co-operative action that has persisted in some dramatic manifestation of itself, an individual may now know that he might gain very exceptional opportunity for some conception of his own.

## PRACTICAL STATUS

The moon's regularity of movement is not precise, since it's daily motion varies by some four degrees from slowest to fastest. Its transits through the signs are of very short duration, ranging from two days to nearly three days. This means that what they reveal may be very fleeting, ephemeral factors of public interest and broad emotional responsiveness. This would mean the general climate of experience, as reflected in an individual emphasis of temperament.

THE MOON WHILE MOVING THROUGH ARIES reveals a prevailing emphasis of ASPIRATION, or outreach to accomplishment, strengthened by a preceding activation of pertinent SYMPATHY now able to stimulate a fresh VIRILITY. A conscious awareness of these lunar rhythms can be very helpful. Thus, if there has been an identifiable and special rapport with others at this moment, an individual can know that he stands at a threshold of some marked personal opportunity in self-expression.

THE MOON WHILE MOVING THROUGH TAURUS reveals a prevailing emphasis of VIRILITY, or unusual energy of self-expression, strengthened by a preceding activation of some particular ASPIRATION now able to contribute significantly to an effective VIVIFICATION. A conscious awareness of these lunar rhythms can be very helpful. Thus, if there has been an identifiable and special concern over goals ahead at this moment, an individual can know that he stands at a threshold of gratifying new power in self-advancement.

THE MOON WHILE MOVING THROUGH GEMINI reveals a prevailing emphasis of VIVIFICATION, or success in special quickening of relevant elements of current reality, strengthened by a preceding activiation of needed VIRILITY now able to gain a proper EXPANSION of effort. A conscious awareness of these lunar rhythms can be very helpful. Thus, if there has been an indentifiable and exceptional energizing of interest and action with very rewarding results at this moment, an individual can know that he stands at a threshold of perhaps remarkable developments of practical adroitness.

THE MOON WHILE MOVING THROUGH CANCER reveals a prevailing emphasis on EXPANSION of his capacities, or perhaps of a definite overall growth strengthened by a preceding activation of VIVIFICATION, or general adroitness now able to cultivate a very genuine ASSURANCE. A conscious awareness of these lunar rhythms can be very helpful. Thus, if there has been an identifiable quickening of various potentials to some profitable use at this moment, an individual can know that he stands at a threshold of possible exceptional enlargement of his general potentials.

THE MOON WHILE MOVING THROUGH LEO reveals a prevailing emphasis of ASSURANCE, or man's properly well-grounded self-orientation, strengthened by a preceding activation of the necessary expansion of growth now able contribute to a genuine ASSIMILATION of all pertinent elements in experience. A conscious awareness of these lunar rhythms can be very helpful. Thus if, at this moment, there has been an identifiable and thoroughly gratifying spread of effort and concern over pertinent matters of any sort, an indiviudal can know that he stands at a threshold of, perhaps, new and very effective self-confidence.

THE MOON WHILE MOVING THROUGH VIRGO reveals a prevailing emphasis of ASSIMILATION, or the human capacity for building the varying essence of circumstances into the actual fiber of self, strengthened by a preceding activation of ASSURANCE now able to establish EQUIVALENCE in any or all reality. A conscious awareness of these lunar rhythms can be very helpful. Thus, if there has been an identifiable, and possibly dramatic, demonstration of the efficacy of self-confidence at this moment, an individual can know that he stands at a threshold of significant recognition of his special competence in the ordering of daily affairs.

THE MOON WHILE MOVING THROUGH LIBRA reveals a pre-

vailing emphasis of EQUIVALENCE, or balance in the fundamental structure of reality, strengthened by a preceding
activation of ASSIMILATION. These are now able to contribute to CREATIVITY with the capacity to manipulate the basic
makeup of all things. A conscious awareness of these lunar
rhythms can be very helpful. Thus, if there has been an
identifiable and exceptional realigning of things which had
been confused or worrisome, an individual can know that
he stands at a threshold of significant involvement in matters of wide importance.

THE MOON WHILE MOVING THROUGH SCORPIO reveals a prevailing emphasis of CREATIVITY, the uninhibited capacity for
restructuring the fundamental nature of almost anything,
strengthened by a preceding activation of EQUIVALENCE now
able to build up man's unique gift of ADMINISTRATION. A
conscious awareness of these lunar rhythms can be very
helpful. Thus, if there has been an identifiable and outstanding instance of effective balancing or harmonizing of
basic elements of real pertinence at this moment, an individual can know that he stands at a threshold of a dramatic
chance for finding solutions in affairs of consequence.

THE MOON WHILE MOVING THROUGH SAGITTARIUS reveals a
prevailing emphasis of ADMINISTRATION, or skill in distribution, strengthened by a preceding activation of CREATIVITY,
a transforming capacity now able to develop a reliable
DISCRIMINATION in ultimate results. A conscious awareness
of these lunar rhythms can be very helpful. Thus, if there
has been an identifiable, significantly creative development
in any special context at the moment, an individual can
know that he stands at the threshold of rewarding recognition throughout the given area of his immediate concern.

THE MOON WHILE MOVING THROUGH CAPRICORN reveals a
prevailing emphasis of DISCRIMINATION, or practical judgment, strengthened by a preceding activation of ADMIN-
ISTRATION able to contribute to an effective LOYALTY or
alignment with worthwhile policies and people. A conscious
awareness of these lunar rhythms can be very helpful.
Thus, if there has been a pertinent and outstanding
demonstration of real leadership in some vital instance at

this moment, the individual can know that he stands at a threshold of an unusual opportunity for legal or social judgment and enduring self-establishment.

THE MOON WHILE MOVING THROUGH AQUARIUS reveals prevailing emphasis of LOYALTY, or exceptionally worthwhile associations and affiliations in life. This is strengthened by a preceding activation of DISCRIMINATION now able to enrich all human relationships by a more personal SYMPATHY or concern. A conscious awareness of these lunar rhythms can be very helpful. Thus, if there has been dramatic evidence of extraordinary good sense in some major crisis at this moment, an individual can know that he stands at a threshold of striking opportunity to bring himself and his fellows into effective rapport or cohesive unity.

THE MOON WHILE MOVING THROUGH PISCES reveals a prevailing emphasis of SYMPATHY strengthened by a preceding activation of LOYALTY, or tangible and continuing association in mutual rapport now able to encourage every pertinent ASPIRATION or general outreach. A conscious awareness of these lunar rhythms can be very helpful. Thus, if there has been some striking manifestation of group integrity or special devotion to some movement by someone of prominence at this moment, an individual can know that he stands at the threshold of wide and effective influence among his fellows.

# PART III

# PERSONAL ASTROLOGY BY USE OF A HOROSCOPE

## Chapter Five
## *DYNAMIC HOROSCOPY*

The horoscope is a chart of the heavens showing the two great circles of the earth's motion, or (1) the zodiac representing the orbit it traverses annually and, (2) the celestial equator it marks out in its daily turning on its axis, as these are located relative to the terrestrial horizon that, at a moment of birth or event, is carried out into the celestial sphere to establish astrology's symbolical and familiar wheel. The planes of the two great cycles lie slantwise in their relation to each other, as can be seen by diagram. The twelve houses of the horoscope, to which very little attention is necessary in this specialized technique, are almost universally shown by printed or drawn solid lines. The horizon, creating the ascendant and descendant, is usually represented by the horizontal line in the wheel. Conversely, the zodiac is not indicated at all by its circle, but in the diagram here its circle is sketched in by dotted line to illustrate the fundamental relationship.

Zodiacal position is commonly indicated by notation of sign, degree and minute of arc at the cusp or boundary of each house, and also at the position of each planet and any other significators. The house cusps can be shown by even degree only, or giving the exact seconds of arc as well. The sun's position is usually given specifically, showing degree, minutes and seconds of arc.

The whole scheme of it can be seen in the completed horoscope of Richard Nixon, to which particular attention will be given in the following pages. It must be realized that normal progress, or motion, is clockwise in the houses (as planets rising in the morning) and counterclockwise in the zodiac (as planets moving from Aries into Taurus) in the established horoscopic diagramming.

## CHART
### The Usual Form of the Horoscope

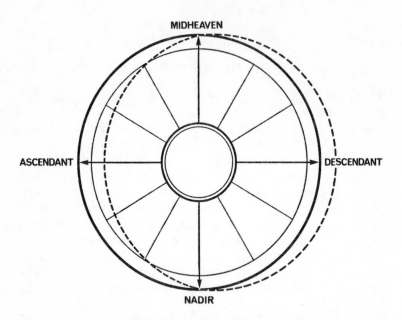

When it comes to the use of the horoscope it is important
to remember that there are two entirely different areas of
interpretation, and that these, at no point, should ever be
confused with each other. Certainly they should never be
considered together. In the case of the native, or subject, of
the astrological analysis, there is first of all (1) what he is at
birth and what thereafter remains unchanged in the substance of himself and then, (2) what he continually develops
and maintains in the living, progressive — or perhaps re-
gressive — unfoldment of this potentiality of himself
through the course of his years. With his great sheaf of
intrinsic and characteristic strains or channels of capacity, it
is beyond all possibility that all of them would unfold in
precisely the same way at the same time. One person may
favor muscle and another intelligence, and which it might
be cannot be predetermined for a creature endowed with

free will and buffeted about in the tides of unpredictable circumstances. Since the outstanding traits of character can be identified in their differentiation at birth by the natures of the planets, it obviously is possible to chart their subsequent shifts and manifestations in at least a general fashion.

What is needed, therefore, is the sharply different technique identified loosely as the progressions; these include the transits which are the special concern of this particular textbook. In order to help keep the attention on the fact that it is working in the dynamic perspective, special key phrases can be employed for identifying the planets in this form of their delineation. These are the ACTIVITY-FACETS, and this employment of keywords and key phrases has been explained and illustrated from the very beginning of this exposition.

It may seem to be a most incomplete procedure to select a certain few of man's most characteristic traits of dynamic manifestations for a general judgment of his progressing or regressing actions and current state of affairs. Yet, an employer interviewing an applicant for a position, or a young lady seriously considering marriage to a likely young man, or a student in college contemplating his own best preparation for his future line of work, cannot possibly take more than a very few representative factors into account. If more is attempted the general level of relevance is lowered, and wrong choices become easier. In fact, it has proven very effective to concentrate astrological attention in these ten easily demarked modes of progressive self-expression. They have proven to be highly characteristic manifestations of life's overall and actually illimitable divisions of labor.

## Chapter Six
# *LIFE'S DIVISIONS*
# *OF LABOR*

BASIC ATTITUDE is the activity-facet of Mercury, and in horoscopic progression it charts the general, or overall, presentation by an individual to his fellows and the world at large. Here MENTALITY dramatizes the prevailing image in mind or self-realization. This inwardly is what there may be of self-confidence; outwardly it is common mannerism and everyday role playing.

NATURAL DRIVE is the activity-facet of the sun, and in horoscopic progression it charts the dominant and disciplined momentum of any person's conscious course. Here PURPOSE dramatizes the core stability of selfhood, no matter how superficially disordered. This, inwardly, can be at least some little flicker of ambition, and outwardly it is man's inability to surrender any last shred of dignity.

BASIC SENSITIVITY is the activity-facet of Venus, and in horoscopic progression it charts man's fundamental and necessary rapport with his environment and so his practical capacity to make use of its potentials. Here ACQUISITIVENESS dramatizes the everyday embellishment of selfhood. Inwardly this is self-gratification, and outwardly it is self-cultivation that often, at worst, is largely at the expense of others.

BASIC EXCITATION is the activity-facet of Mars, and in horoscopic progression it charts the competitive necessity of all life, the need for any living creature to stir up reality in order to remain any part of it. Here INITIATIVE dramatizes human existence as a continual doing. This, inwardly, is the steady utilization of energy that permits self to be itself, and outwardly it is the sheer trial and error that creates conscious being.

NASCENT CONSISTENCY is the activity-facet of Jupiter, and in horoscopic progression it is the ever-being-born fidelity to self-difference that constitutes genuine personality. Here ENTHUSIASM dramatizes the uncompromising fluidity of the more or less chosen experience of mankind. This, inwardly, is an extradimensional selfhood, as far above the animals in the scope of it, and outwardly it is the full sweep of thoroughly personal existence.

NASCENT INTEGRITY is the activity-facet of Saturn, and in horoscopic progression it is the ever-being-born fidelity to the prevailing structures of reality that essentially are the foundation of all wisdom. Here SENSITIVENESS dramatizes the remarkable ability of man to remain aware of relevances of every possible sort of his conscious ongoing. Inwardly this is the pyramiding rewards of what is learned through experience, and outwardly it is an ever-expanding good commonsense.

NASCENT INDIVIDUALISM is the activity-facet of Uranus, and in horoscopic progression it is the ever-being-born realization of man's new dimensions of life in the totally unique present day world. Here, INDEPENDENCE dramatizes modern destiny as the release, finally, of unlimited, and long suppressed human potentialities. This, inwardly, is encouragement to the exercise of one's original capacity, and outwardly is a widening fellowship in free-wheeling accomplishment.

NASCENT RESPONSIBILITY is the activity-facet of Neptune. In horoscopic progression it is the ever-being-born establishment of new challenge to human life in its worldwide socioeconomic organization. Here OBLIGATION dramatizes modern destiny as bringing men increasingly more closely together, sharing mutual concerns for everyday welfare. This, inwardly, is the new social conscience, and outwardly it is uncompromising advancement of group co-operation.

NASCENT ENLIGHTENMENT is the activity-facet of Pluto. In horoscopic progression it is the ever-being-born realization of this new age of mankind in which individual differences integrate in an ultimately classless and thoroughly fluid society. Here OBSESSION dramatizes its developing universal and infinitely varied self-commitment.

This, inwardly, is high vision of the world of unceasing human promise; outwardly it is the challenging force of fulfillments — actual and anticipatory — of the extraordinary potentials only beginning to reveal themselves.

NATURAL INVOLVEMENT is the activity-facet of the moon and, in horoscopic progression, it charts the concomitant and ultimately reconciled trends of public life and general, fundamental human affairs. Here FEELING, or emotional concern, dramatizes the scope of external reality of which an individual can take advantage. Inwardly, this is his struggle to master himself, and outwardly it is his effort to find or help sustain the actual and ultimate stability of the world at large and to align himself with it.

The dynamic (progressive) astrology primarily charts or measures the development, or lack of it, of the various character traits which make up the living totality of the individual. Obviously each of these sets its own pace, and so they cannot often be seen as significant at the same moment or in the same place. In consequence, and most essentially for effective judgment, each such separate trait must be considered in its own special context of significance. In the delineation of the transits in their particular activity-facets, the technique follows along the lines already presented in the preceding pages as stimulating impacts on the individual natal planets. But the indication now is not for everybody, but rather very specifically for a single individual. In that instance the transit must be within proper orb, or boundary of effectiveness, in arriving at the zodiacal position of some planet in a horoscope. This means within sixty minutes or a single degree of the zodiac on each side of the exact natal place of the activated planet.

What is meant by activation is an identification of that natal planet's momentary specific significance in its own personal cycle. The activating is within the general cyclic manifestation of the activity-facet, while that is operating in connection with everybody in the overall perspective. Sometimes, but not too often, the transiting planet of the activity-facet will change its direction or motion from direct to retrograde or vice versa. If this happens within the one-degree orb on either side of the natal planet it is activating, the indication may be dramatically intensified and thus the challenge to an individual exceptionally expanded. The heightened significance, moreover, can be such that a balancing and equally important quickening can become effective at a precisely opposite point in the zodiac. In such an instance the consideration should be given to any natal planet then quickened, whether additionally or only by itself in the given case. The sun never retrogrades but when it has special accentuation, such as a solar eclipse, its heightened indication is considered in the same manner.

## TABLE E
## THE ACTIVITY-FACETS

| | | | |
|---|---|---|---|
| Mercury | Basic attitude | Saturn | Nascent integrity |
| The sun | Natural drive | Uranus | Nascent Individualism |
| Venus | Basic sensitivity | Neptune | Nascent responsibility |
| Mars | Basic excitation | Pluto | Nascent enlightenment |
| Jupiter | Nascent consistency | The moon | Natural involvement |

## *BASIC ATTITUDE*

TRANSITING MERCURY, passing over the zodiacal sign and degree occupied by MERCURY AT BIRTH, indicates a possible stimulation of the native's MENTALITY in that area of his basic attitude. This means an important realization in some phase of his understanding, such as can help his general influence. The transit usually happens every year and if, on any recent occasion of it, there was striking manifestation of his unusual influence among others, there is likelihood now of further self-effectiveness. If not, there may be a need for a much greater overall interest in life. If transiting Mercury becomes stationary at this point, the indication may be dramatically intensified.

TRANSITING MERCURY, passing over the zodiacal sign and degree occupied by the SUN AT BIRTH, indicates a possible stimulation of the native's PURPOSE in that area of his basic attitude. This means a definite strengthening of ambition in some special line, such as may commandeer vital assistance from his fellows. The transit usually happens every year and if, on any recent occasion of it, there was some incident of dramatic encouragement for him, there is a likelihood of another real boost to progress now. If not, there may be a need for a more definite self-assertion. If transiting Mercury becomes stationary at this point, the indication may be much more significant.

TRANSITING MERCURY, passing over the zodiacal sign and degree occupied by VENUS AT BIRTH, indicates a possible stimulation of the native's ACQUISITIVENESS in that area of his basic attitude. This means some very exceptional gain in resources, or sudden unlocking of potentials for furthering self-interest, as a new factor in basic attitude. The transit usually happens every year and if, on any recent occasion of it, there was good luck of this order, there is likelihood of another windfall of sorts. If not, there may be a need for a sharper sense of rapport with current circumstances. If transiting Mercury becomes stationary at this point, the indication is more vital.

TRANSITING MERCURY, passing over the zodiacal sign and degree occupied by MARS AT BIRTH, indicates a possible stimulation of the native's INITIATIVE in that area of his basic attitude. This means an unusual opening for his special capacity of personal competence, such as can reinforce his basic attitude effectively. The transit usually happens every year and if, on any recent occasion of it, he was able to take very significant action, there is likelihood of another fortuitous opening. If not, there may be a need for more get-up-and-go in daily living. If transiting Mercury becomes stationary at this point, the testimony may be of much greater importance.

TRANSITING MERCURY, passing over the zodiacal sign and degree occupied by JUPITER AT BIRTH, indicates a possible stimulation of the native's ENTHUSIASM in that area of his basic attitude. This means some very striking manifestation of this characteristic of his personality, such as establishes or maintains him in some special esteem of his fellows. The transit usually happens every year and if, on some recent occasion of it, he performed an important function with real distinction, there is likelihood of effective repetition. If transiting Mercury becomes stationary at this point, the challenge to him may be very great.

TRANSITING MERCURY, passing over the zodiacal sign and degree occupied by SATURN AT BIRTH, indicates a possible stimulation of the native's OBLIGATION in that area of his basic attitude. This means exceptional awareness of the vital relevance in some current crisis, which can contribute to effective control or exploitation of the basic potential. The transit usually happens every year and, if on a recent occasion of it he demonstrated his capacity very decisively, there is likelihood of a real chance to do so again. If not, there is need for a greater alertness in daily living. If transiting Mercury becomes stationary at this point, the challenge is greatly heightened.

TRANSITING MERCURY, passing over the zodiacal sign and degree occupied by URANUS AT BIRTH, indicates a possible stimulation of the native's INDEPENDENCE in that area of his basic attitude. This means a dramatically idealistic self-assertion in current crisis, such as can hold him apart from the mediocrities of his more conventionally conditioned fellows. The transit usually happens every year and if, on some recent occasion of it, he clearly revealed some unique competence of the moment, there is a good chance now of a repeated performance. If not, there is sharp need for a heightened interest in daily living. If transiting Mercury becomes stationary at this point, the indication is strengthened very vitally.

TRANSITING MERCURY, passing over the zodiacal sign and degree occupied by NEPTUNE AT BIRTH, indicates a possible stimulation of the native's OBLIGATION in that area of his basic attitude. This means a marked self-discipline, or effective social consciousness, in all matters of crisis concerning his fellows. The transit usually happens every year and if, on a recent occasion of it, he gave some dramatic demonstration of a broad or general interest in humanity, there is likelihood of further opportunity along this line. If not, he may have real need for broader horizons. If transiting Mercury becomes stationary at this point, the indication can have exceptionally wide significance.

TRANSITING MERCURY, passing over the zodiacal sign and degree occupied by PLUTO AT BIRTH, indicates a possible stimulation of the native's OBSESSION in that area of his basic attitude. This means exceptional self-dedication, or a complete alignment with objectives, that can thus typify human personality in the new age of mankind. The transit usually happens every year and if, on a recent occasion, the fact of this obsessive interest had dramatically rewarding consequences for the native, there is likely to be a chance for another successful manifestation of the interest at the present time. If not, there may be great need for personal re-dedication. If transiting Mercury becomes stationary at this point, the indication can be far more significant.

TRANSITING MERCURY, passing over the zodiacal sign and degree occupied by the MOON AT BIRTH, indicates a possible stimulation of the active's FEELING in that area of his basic attitude. This means a definite strengthening of his emotions or capacity for intimate relationship with others. The transit usually happens every year and if, on any recent occasion, he stood up in unswerving fidelity to his own desires and so won others over to himself strikingly, this tonic of experience may well have a very significant reoccurance. If not, there may be need for a warmer self-expression. If transiting Mercury becomes stationary at this point, the indication may have exceptional breadth.

## NATURAL DRIVE

THE TRANSITING SUN, passing over the zodiacal sign and degree occupied by MERCURY AT BIRTH, indicates a possible stimulation of the native's MENTALITY in special contribution to the natural drive. This means a reason for acting. The transit happens regularly every year. If, on any previous occasion, a gratifying and new understanding of customary everyday procedures was gained, there is likelihood of additional comprehension of the life-drives at this point; if not, it may be necessary to climb up out of a needless rut. If the sun should be in solar eclipse at this point, the indication is greatly intensified.

THE TRANSITING SUN, passing over the zodiacal sign and degree occupied by THE SUN AT BIRTH, indicates a possible stimulation of the native's PURPOSE, a special contribution to the natural drive of conscious human existence. This means simple pressure for acting. The transit happens every year regularly and if, on the preceding occasion, there was a dramatic upsurge of energy or the joy of existence, there can again be this self-renewal. If not, life may have to be regrasped effectively. If the sun should be in solar eclipse at this point, the indication becomes far more vital.

THE TRANSITING SUN, passing over the zodiacal sign and degree occupied by VENUS AT BIRTH, indicates a possible stimulation of the native's ACQUISITIVENESS in a special contribution to the natural drive of conscious human existence. This means reward for acting. The transit happens regularly every year and if, on the previous occasion, there were unusual gains of physical or psychological nature as the result of accentuated effort, there is likelihood of real access to a greater wealth of reality at this time; if not, life needs much refinement. If the sun should be in solar eclipse at this point, the indication has crucial import.

THE TRANSITING SUN, passing over the zodiacal sign and degree occupied by MARS AT BIRTH, indicates a possible stimulation of the native's INITIATIVE in special contribution to the natural drive of conscious human existence. This means reliability in acting. The transit happens regularly every year and if, on the previous occasion, there was a crucial taking over of something to be done and so an inauguration of continuous activity, there is likelihood now of parallel accomplishment. If not, life needs a thorough-going dynamic challenge. If the sun should be in solar eclipse at this point, the indication can be exceptionally vital.

THE TRANSITING SUN, passing over the zodiacal sign and degree occupied by JUPITER AT BIRTH, indicates a possible stimulation of the native's ENTHUSIASM in special contribution to the natural drive of conscious human existence. This means significance in acting, as when personality is involved. The transit happens every year regularly and if, on the preceding occasion there was a striking richness of achievement, there is likelihood of repetition at this time. If not, life is shown lackluster and in need of zest. If the sun should be in solar eclipse at this point, the indication can be dramatic.

THE TRANSITING SUN, passing over the zodiacal sign and degree occupied by SATURN AT BIRTH, indicates a possible stimulation of the native's SENSITIVENESS in special contribution to the natural drive of conscious human existence. This means astuteness in acting or when wisdom is involved. The transit happens every year regularly and if, on the prior occasion, there were highly dramatic solutions clearing the way for real accomplishment, there is likelihood of parallel surmounting of obstacles for high achievement now. If not, current living may be seriously inept. If the sun should be in solar eclipse at this point, the indication is intensified.

THE TRANSITING SUN passing over the zodiacal sign and degree occupied by URANUS AT BIRTH, indicates a possible stimulation of the native's INDEPENDENCE in special contribution to the natural drive of conscious human existence. This means uninhibited acting, or shows the new group dimensions of mankind are involved. The transit happens every year regularly and if, on the prior occasion there were fresh developments of great worth and without conventional conditioning, there is likelihood of even more original ones at the present time. If not, the old order remains. If the sun should be in solar eclipse at this point, the issue of the moment becomes greater.

THE TRANSITING SUN, passing over the zodiacal sign and degree occupied by NEPTUNE AT BIRTH, indicates a possible stimulation of the native's OBLIGATION in special contribution to the natural drive of conscious human existence. This means conscientious acting, or that the new group responsibilities of all people are involved. The transit happens regularly every year and if, on the preceding occasion there were brilliant new accomplishments in human welfare, there is likelihood of even broader achievement now. If not, the older rivalries persist. If the sun should be in solar eclipse at this point, the indication has far greater import.

THE TRANSITING SUN, passing over the zodiacal sign and degree occupied by PLUTO AT BIRTH, indicates a possible stimulus of the native's OBSESSION in special contribution to the natural drive of conscious human existence. This means irrevocable acting, or that the new group dedications of mankind are involved. The transit happens every year regularly and if, on the prior occasion there were some splendid examples of binding people to worthwhile ends, there is likelihood of effective transcendent effort now. If not, the outworn conceptions retain allegiance. If the sun should be in solar eclipse at this point, the indication becomes vital.

THE TRANSITING SUN, passing over the zodiacal sign and degree occupied by THE MOON AT BIRTH, indicates a possible stimulus of the native's FEELING in special contribution to the natural drive of conscious human existence. This means spontaneous acting, in response to others who are concerned in any way. The transit happens regularly and if, on the previous occasion, there was high rapport with the masses in some vital everyday project, there is likelihood of popular and worthwhile development of parallel scope at the present time. If not, life may be lethargic and need quickening. If the sun should be in solar eclipse at this point, the indication gains real significance.

## BASIC SENSITIVITY

TRANSITING VENUS, passing over the zodiacal sign and degree occupied by MERCURY AT BIRTH, indicates a possible stimulation of the native's MENTALITY in the refinement of his basic sensitivity. This means a reason for self-cultivation or even self-indulgence. The transit usually happens about once a year and if, on any recent occasion of it, there has been an especially dramatic accomplishment through general appearance and availability of resources, there is likelihood of similar further development. If not, there is need for definite self-enhancement. If transiting Venus becomes stationary at its impact, the indication is intensified.

TRANSITING VENUS, passing over the zodiacal sign and degree occupied by THE SUN AT BIRTH, indicates a possible stimulation of the native's PURPOSE in the refinement of his basic sensitivity. This means concern over self-appearance and self-establishment as a fundamental basis of existence. The transit usually happens about once a year and if, meeting any of these ends has brought sharp manifestation of their effectiveness, there is likelihood of even greater advance in self-cultivation now. If not, this interest may degenerate into idle vanity. If transiting Venus becomes stationary at this point, the indication may have more potential than realized.

TRANSITING VENUS, passing over the zodiacal sign and degree occupied by VENUS AT BIRTH, indicates a possible stimulation of the native's ACQUISITIVENESS in the refinement of his basic sensitivity. This means pure self-appreciation, or an expectation of almost everything from everybody. The transit usually happens about once a year and if, on any recent occasion, there has been unusual reward for catering to the self, there is likelihood of helpful repetition of it. If not, there may be insufficient effort to maintain the rapport with things generally. If transiting Venus becomes stationary at this point, the natural self-exaltation may have exceptional call to justify itself.

TRANSITING VENUS, passing over the zodiacal sign and degree occupied by MARS AT BIRTH, indicates a possible stimulation of the native's INITIATIVE in the refinement of his basic sensitivity. This means exaggerated self-expression, or some specialized impulse of the esthetic nature. The transit usually happens about once a year and if, on a recent occasion of it, there was highly imaginative drama of self-unfoldment, there is likelihood of reinforcement of this at the present moment. It not, life is not appreciated on a level high enough for any refined individuality. If transiting Venus becomes stationary at this point, the indication becomes more definitely significant.

TRANSITING VENUS, passing over the zodiacal sign and degree occupied by JUPITER AT BIRTH, indicates a possible stimulation of the native's ENTHUSIASM in the refinement of his basic sensitivity. This means thoroughness of self-realization, or pride of appearance becoming pride of influence on others. The transit usually happens about once a year and if, on some recent occasion of it, there was credit for special personal accomplishment, there is likelihood of further recognition at this time. If not, any real participation in life is being neglected. If transiting Venus becomes stationary at this point, the indication can have exceptional individual importance.

TRANSITING VENUS, passing over the zodiacal sign and degree occupied by SATURN AT BIRTH, indicates a possible stimulation of the native's SENSITIVENESS in the refinement of his basic sensitivity. This means exceptional alertness in self-realization, or capacity for recognizing current relevances of the individual activity. The transit usually happens about once a year and if, on a recent instance of it there was a dramatic grasp of momentary opportunity for self-expression, there is likelihood of similar challenge through events at the present moment. If not, a lack of real attention to everyday eventuations must be met. If transiting Venus becomes stationary at this point, self-reorientation becomes especially vital.

TRANSITING VENUS, passing over the zodiacal sign and degree occupied by URANUS AT BIRTH, indicates a possible stimulation of the native's INDEPENDENCE in the refinement of his basic sensitivity. This means pure adventure in self-realization, or continual trial and error in self-discovery. The transit usually happens about once a year and if, on a preceding instance of it there was exceptional success in experimental living, there is likelihood of repetition in perhaps broader scope at this time. If not, there is needless limitation to be overcome. If transiting Venus becomes stationary at this point, the indication can be significantly strengthened.

TRANSITING VENUS, passing over the zodiacal sign and degree occupied by NEPTUNE AT BIRTH, indicates a possible stimulus of the native's OBLIGATION in the refinement of his basic sensitivity. This means vital responsibility perhaps for all mankind collectively, or special orientation above normal everyday affairs. The transit usually happens about once a year and if, on a prior occasion of it there was high achievement in serving some significant mass action, there is likelihood of a greater call to service now. If not, there is need of broader realization in general. If transiting Venus becomes stationary at this point, the challenge is greatly increased.

TRANSITING VENUS, passing over the zodiacal sign and degree occupied by PLUTO AT BIRTH, indicates a possible stimulation of the native's OBSESSION in the refinement of his basic sensitivity. This means total self-dedication in an enlightened dimension of some sort, or alignment, somehow, to special human values. The transit usually happens about once a year and if, on a previous instance of it there was accomplishment of remarkable benefit to men everywhere, there is likelihood of similar contribution at the present time. It not, life needs special illumination. If transiting Venus becomes stationary at this point, the indication is much more vital.

TRANSITING VENUS, passing over the zodiacal sign and degree occupied by THE MOON AT BIRTH, indicates a possible stimulation of the native's FEELING in the refinement of his basic sensitivity. This means continual enlistment of others for the furthering of his fundamental self-appearance and self-establishment. The transit usually happens about once a year and if, on a prior occasion of it there was dramatic success in gaining public support for himself, there is likelihood of further achievement of this. If not, life needs imaginative exaltation in this case. If transiting Venus becomes stationary at this point, the moment's potentiality is intensified.

## BASIC EXCITATION

TRANSITING MARS, passing over the zodiacal sign and degree occupied by MERCURY AT BIRTH, indicates the likely enlistment of the native's MENTALITY in challenging his basic excitation into productive manifestation of itself. This means a reason for the current phase of the continual doing that constitutes any living reality. The transit happens at intervals of up to some two years. If at a previous occurrence it was possible to find the overall course of individual life adequately reasonable, it would be practical to make sound future plans at this time. If transiting Mars should become stationary at this point, the indication is sharpened.

TRANSITING MARS, passing over the zodiacal sign and degree occupied by THE SUN AT BIRTH, indicates the likely enlistment of the native's PURPOSE in channeling his basic excitation into productive manifestation of itself. This means a definite ambition that can sustain the continual doing such as constitutes any living reality. The transit happens at intervals of up to some two years. If at any prior instance there was significant accomplishment to encourage the particular effort, it woutd be practical to adopt this course for future development. If transiting Mars should become stationary at this point, the indication may be all the more significant.

TRANSITING MARS, passing over the zodiacal sign and degree occupied by VENUS AT BIRTH, indicates a likely enlistment of the native's ACQUISITIVENESS in channeling his basic excitation into productive manifestation of itself. This means a rapport with environmental potentials of particular aptness for the continual doing that constitutes any living reality. The transit happens at intervals up to some two years. If, at some previous occurrence of it, there were enduring results from efforts in the circumstances at the time, it would be practical to repeat the effort now. If transiting Mars should become stationary at this point, the indication is unusually vital.

TRANSITING MARS, passing over the zodiacal sign and degree occupied by MARS AT BIRTH, indicates the likely enlistment of the native's INITIATIVE in channeling his basic excitation into productive manifestation of itself. This means an encouragement of the continual freewheeling enterprise into endless demonstration of its ramifying possibilities from which to make selection. The transit happens at intervals up to some two years. If at some prior instance certain measures have had high success, it would be practical to keep repeating them. If transiting Mars should become stationary at this point, the indications would be exceptionally significant.

TRANSITING MARS, passing over the zodiacal sign and degree occupied by JUPITER AT BIRTH, indicated the likely enlistment of the native's ENTHUSIASM in channeling his basic excitation into productive manifestation of itself. This means an employment of highly personal factors in the essential doing that constitutes any living reality. The transit happens at intervals up to some two years. If at a previous occurrence there was a remarkable demonstration of the effectiveness of the personality, it would be practical to proceed again in the same manner. If transiting Mars should become stationary at this point, the indication is especially strengthened.

TRANSITING MARS, passing over the zodiacal sign and degree occupied by SATURN AT BIRTH, indicates the likely enlistment of the native's SENSITIVENESS in channeling his basic excitation into productive manifestation of itself. This means recourse to the simple awareness of immediate relevancies in the essential doing that constitutes any living reality. The transit happens at intervals up to some two years. If at a prior instance there was perhaps extraordinary success through special adroitness, it would be practical to repeat the former procedure. If transiting Mars should become stationary at this point, indication should be strong indeed.

TRANSITING MARS, passing over the zodiacal sign and degree occupied by URANUS AT BIRTH, indicates the likely enlistment of the native's INDEPENDENCE in channeling his basic excitation into productive manifestation of itself. This means an encouragement of the totally unconditioned doing that helps establish the new age of mankind. The transit happens at intervals up to some two years. If in a prior case there was a remarkable demonstration of the efficacy of the new individual freedom of man, it would be practical to shape current response along the same lines. If transiting Mars should become stationary at this point, the indication has extra pertinence.

TRANSITING MARS, passing over the zodiacal sign and degree occupied by NEPTUNE AT BIRTH, indicates the likely enlistment of the native's OBLIGATION in channeling his basic excitation into productive manifestation of itself. This means simple concern for the welfare of man, marked in the essential doing that constitutes any living reality. The transit happens at intervals up to some two years. If in a preceding instance there was dramatic demonstration of a capacity to operate co-operatively through the civilized culture, it would be practical to adopt this course now. If transiting Mars should become stationary at this point, the indication is particularly intensified.

TRANSITING MARS passing over the zodiacal sign and degree occupied by PLUTO AT BIRTH, indicates the likely enlistment of the native's OBSESSION in channeling his basic excitation into productive manifestation of itself. This means special encouragement of total dedication in service to the living reality of the new age now perhaps well launched. The transit happens at intervals up to some two years. If its prior occurrence provided unusual dramatization of these new values and their power, it would be practical to hold to this course. If transiting Mars should become stationary at this point, the indication is most vital.

TRANSITING MARS, passing over the zodiacal sign and degree occupied by THE MOON AT BIRTH, indicates the likely enlistment of the native's FEELING in channeling his basic excitation into productive manifestation of itself. This means a definite involvement or wholly individual participation in the continual doing that has established and now maintains the living reality of immediate pertinence. The transit happens at intervals up to some two years. If its preceding instance was marked by dramatic development of public support for some vital new contribution to current human development, a great new step forward may be possible. If transiting Mars should become stationary at this point, the indication gains a double force.

## NASCENT CONSISTENCY

TRANSITING JUPITER, passing over the zodiacal sign and degree occupied by MERCURY AT BIRTH, indicates the native's
personal balance, with his own kind, through MENTALITY —
re-establishment of a distinctive selfhood in comparison
with the others around him. This means the simple clinging
to difference as the essence of identity. The transit occurs
about every twelve years and if, at a previous occurrence
there was striking recognition of the personality, there is
now unusual opportunity for more gratifying self-orien-
tations. A station of Jupiter at this point intensifies the
challenge to broader dimensions of ongoing.

TRANSITING JUPITER, passing over the zodiacal sign and
degree occupied by THE SUN AT BIRTH, identifies the native's
personal balance, with his own kind, through ACQUIS-
ITIVENESS — the endless competitions in life for the possessions or relations that certify selfhood. This means the
unceasing effort of the individual to keep others in their
place around him. The transit occurs about every twelve
years and if, on some previous instance there was dramatic
accomplishment in maintaining his position in a real crisis,
there now can be special opportunity for great self-advancement. A station of Jupiter at this point intensifies the
indication of some such vital challenge.

TRANSITING JUPITER, passing over the zodiacal sign and
degree occupied by VENUS AT BIRTH, identifies the native's
personal balance, with his own kind, through ACQUIS-
ITIVENESS — the endless competitions in life for the possessions or relations that certify selfhood. This means the
unceasing effort of the individual to keep others in their
place around him. The transit occurs about every twelve
years and if, on some previous instance there was dramatic
accomplishment in maintaining his position in a real crisis,
there now can be special opportunity for great self-
advancement. A station Jupiter at this point intensifies the
indication of some such vital challenge.

TRANSITING JUPITER, passing over the zodiacal sign and

degree occupied by MARS AT BIRTH, identifies the native's personal balance, with his own kind, through INITIATIVE — the characteristic trial-and-error of everyday life in which this balancing is tested constantly. This means the needed improvisation of his personality must never be curtailed. The transit happens about every twelve years and if, at a prior case of it there was real benefit from an uninhibited shift of effort in the given circumstances, there is the chance for something of equal promise. A station of Jupiter at this point intensifies the opportunity.

TRANSITING JUPITER, passing over the zodiacal sign and degree occupied by JUPITER AT BIRTH, identifies the native's personal balance, with his own kind, through ENTHUSIASM — man's capacity for endless, psychological self-projection whenever opportunity offers. This means wholehearted giving of self in any area of interest at some moment of genuine concern. The transit occurs about every twelve years and if, at some prior occurrence there was a dramatic outbreak of temperament that precipitated gratifying and perhaps enduring results, there now can be equal opportunity. A station of Jupiter at this point would heighten the potential.

TRANSITING JUPITER, passing over the zodiacal sign and degree occupied by SATURN AT BIRTH, identifies the native's personal balance, with his own kind, through SENSITIVENESS to the continual, necessary response of all life to the relevancies surrounding it. This means the psychological aliveness of human personality in what ultimately becomes man's wisdom. The transit happens about every twelve years and if, at some previous time of it there was very striking success in a special demonstration of personal intelligence, there can be another valuable example at this time. A station of Jupiter at this point would suggest every intensification of the chance for it.

TRANSITING JUPITER, passing over the zodiacal sign and degree occupied by URANUS AT BIRTH, identifies the native's personal balance, with his own kind, through INDEPENDENCE — the full capacity for unconditioned self-realization in a modern world. This means true originality, or the unlimited chance to preserve self-distinctiveness. The transit occurs about every twelve years and if, at a prior occurrence of it, there were gratifying developments with exceptional, unique handling of the problems involved, there now may be similar opportunity of greater scope. A station of Jupiter at this point would intensify this.

TRANSITING JUPITER, passing over the zodiacal sign and degree occupied by NEPTUNE AT BIRTH, identifies the native's personal balance, with his own kind, through OBLIGATION or the very modern demand that men play their part in the total context of everyday life. This means a complete sharing of life and its responsibilities. The transit happens about every twelve years and if, at a previous instance of it, there was exceptional accomplishment of common benefit by collective action, there may be additional opportunity of the same sort. A station of Jupiter at this point would show increased scope for that.

TRANSITING JUPITER, passing over the zodiacal sign and degree occupied by PLUTO AT BIRTH, identifies the native's personal balance, with his own kind, through OBSESSION or the possibility of one's individuality acting wholly in rapport with his fellows in their common dedication. This means a practical transcendence of the more usual orientations for the sake of more significant accomplishment. The transit occurs about every twelve years and if, at a prior occurrence there had been some spectacular higher achievement, there now could be vital repetition of it. A station of Jupiter at this point would heighten the potential.

TRANSITING JUPITER, passing over the zodiacal sign and degree occupied by THE MOON AT BIRTH, identifies the native's personal balance, with his own kind, through FEELING, or the characteristic responsiveness of the various elements of selfhood to all the ramifications of life. This means his emotional nature and its direct rapport with the immediate environment. The transit happens about every twelve years and if, at a previous instance of it, there was some perhaps dramatic achievement in meeting emergency public demands, there is special opportunity now for another and related accomplishment. A station of Jupiter at this point would intensify the indication.

## NASCENT INTEGRITY

TRANSITING SATURN passing over the zodiacal sign and degree occupied by MERCURY AT BIRTH, indicates the native's personal balance with the world at large through his MENTALITY or tireless orientations as he rectifies these in the light of his own personal experience. This means developing his common sense and ultimately his wisdom. The transit occurs about every twenty-nine years and if, at any occurrence, he achieves some exceptionally dramatic recognition for his judgment or underlying intelligence, he may know that he is mentally effective. If Saturn, in the rare possibility of it, is also stationary at this point, some truly vital potentiality is shown.

TRANSITING SATURN, passing over the zodiacal sign and degree occupied by THE SUN AT BIRTH, indicates the native's personal balance with the world at large through PURPOSE or his blind drive of sheer existence as he shapes this in the light of his own experience. This means developing his competence and ultimately his ambition. The transit occurs about every twenty-nine years and if, at any occurrence he establishes a firm foundation for himself in sudden and dramatic action, he may know that he is effectively competent. If Saturn, in the rare possibility of it, is also stationary at this point, some truly vital steadiness is shown.

TRANSITING SATURN passing over the zodiacal sign and degree occupied by VENUS AT BIRTH, indicates the native's personal balance with the world at large through ACQUISITIVENESS, or his underlying rapport with all things as he makes use of them in the light of his own experience. This means developing his esthetic capacity or practical appreciation. The transit occurs about every twenty-nine years and if, at any occurrence, he gains a dramatic recognition of his self-refinement, he may know that he is essentially his own best mentor. If Saturn, in the rare possibility of it, is also stationary at this point, his truly vital sensibility is shown.

TRANSITING SATURN passing over the zodiacal sign and degree occupied by MARS AT BIRTH, indicates the native's personal balance with the world at large through INITIATIVE, or his capacity for inaugurating and maintaining everyday practicality and perfecting this in the light of his own experience. The transit occurs about every twenty-five years and if, at any occurrence he moves spectacularly to solve extraordinary difficulties in sudden emergency, he learns his true power. If Saturn, in the rare possibility of it, is also stationary at this point, his performance is shown to be of truly high significance.

TRANSITING SATURN, passing over the zodiacal sign and degree occupied by JUPITER AT BIRTH, indicates the native's personal balance with the world at large through ENTHUSIASM or his ability to throw the whole of himself into whatever he does, dominating it in the light of his own experience. This means his sheer honesty of participation in life. The transit occurs about every twenty-nine years and if, at any occurrence he brings a high dignity to some striking accomplishment, he may demonstrate great quality of leadership. If Saturn, in the rare possibility of it, is also stationary at this point, his real stature is revealed.

TRANSITING SATURN, passing over the zodiacal sign and degree occupied by SATURN AT BIRTH, indicates the native's personal balance with the world at large through SENSITIVENESS of his capacity for drawing into himself everything, in essence, in the form of understanding and conscious alertness. This means stark wisdom, ultimately. The transit occurs about every twenty-nine years and if, at any occurrence he demonstrates dramatic intelligence in some particular crisis, he shows the scope of this capacity. If Saturn, in the rare possibility of it, is also stationary at this point, his achievement is shown to have very unusual importance.

TRANSITING SATURN, passing over the zodiacal sign and degree occupied by URANUS AT BIRTH, indicates the native's personal balance with the world at large through

INDEPENDENCE or his uninhibited realization of the nature of things in the scope of modern experience. This means pure freedom of thought, and so, originality of concept. The transit occurs about every twenty-nine years and if, at any occurrence he transcends normal reason in a dramatic incident of incisive brilliance, he demonstrates the intellectual possibilities of the new age of mankind. If Saturn, in the rare possibility of it, is also stationary at this point, his achievement is revealed as, perhaps, of actual pioneer importance.

TRANSITING SATURN, passing over the zodiacal sign and degree occupied by NEPTUNE AT BIRTH, indicates the native's personal balance with the world at large through OBLIGATION, or his uninhibited acceptance of the group responsibility in the new age — this means human welfare. The transit occurs about every twenty-nine years and if, at any occurrence he makes some exceptionally significant contribution to the new trends, he demonstrates the socio-economic and political possibilities of the new age. If Saturn, in the rare possibility of it, is also stationary at this point, his achievement is shown to be of special significance.

TRANSITING SATURN, passing over the zodiacal sign and degree occupied by PLUTO AT BIRTH, indicates the native's personal balance with the world at large through OBSESSION or total self-dedication. This means the new self-sufficiency of organism rather than organizaiton, or the New Age fellowship of man. The transit occurs about every twenty-nine years and, if any occurrence is marked by, perhaps, epochal contribution to the expanding form of human co-operation, he demonstrates his own high potential. If Saturn, in the rare possibility of it, is also stationary at this point, his achievement is revealed as of truly great importance.

TRANSITING SATURN, passing over the zodiacal sign and degree occupied by THE MOON AT BIRTH, indicates the native's personal balance with the world at large through FEELING or the intimate rapport with the immediate details of everyday life. This means simple adjustment to relevancies in the light of personal experience. The transit

occurs about every twenty-nine years and if, on any occurrence it corresponds to some contribution of worthwhile
insight to those with whom he is associating, he may know
that he is genuinely alive. If Saturn, in the rare possibility of
it, is also stationary at this point, his development is very
significant.


## NASCENT INDIVIDUALISM

TRANSITING URANUS, passing over the zodiacal sign and degree occupied by MERCURY AT BIRTH, indicates the native's
heightened individuality in the new age of mankind as
channeled in MENTALITY. This means exceptional realization of his broader modern potentials. The transit occurs
about every eighty-four years — perhaps once in a lifetime.
If, at the moment, he is able to make a distinctive contribution to the understanding of man's new liberties, he may
know that his life has a special significance well worth developing. If Uranus, in the rare possibility of it, is also
stationary at this point, the indication is magnified strikingly.

TRANSITING URANUS, passing over the zodiacal sign and
degree occupied by THE SUN AT BIRTH, indicates the native's
heightened individuality in the new age of mankind as
channeled in PURPOSE. This means unusual driving force in
the manifestation of his broader potentials. The transit
occurs about every eighty-four years — perhaps once in a
lifetime. If he is able, at the moment, to carry out some
special project of new-age significance, he may know that
his efforts are of dramatic value. If Uranus, in the rare
possibility of it, is also stationary at this point, the indication
is greatly magnified.

TRANSITING URANUS, passing over the zodiacal sign and
degree occupied by VENUS AT BIRTH, indicates the native's
heightened individuality in the new age of mankind as
channeled in ACQUISITIVENESS. This means unusual rapport
with, and utilization of, the broader modern potentials.
The transit occurs about every eighty-four years or perhaps

once in a lifetime. If he is able at the moment to capitalize dramatically on the recognition and development of particular unique factors in everyday living, he may know that his efforts have high effectiveness. If Uranus, in the rare possibility of it, is also stationary at this point, the indication is greatly intensified.

TRANSITING URANUS, passing over the zodiacal sign and degree occupied by MARS AT BIRTH, indicates the native's heightened individuality in the new age of mankind as channeled in INITIATIVE. This means exceptional effectiveness in the inauguration and maintenance of especially modern enterprise. The transit occurs about every eighty-four years or perhaps once in a lifetime. If he is able to set up some dramatic demonstration of the new order of things in everyday affairs, he may know that he is operating in a most significant trend. If Uranus, in the rare possibility of it, is also stationary at the moment, the indication is truly magnified.

TRANSITING URANUS, passing over the zodiacal sign and degree occupied by JUPITER AT BIRTH, indicates the native's heightened individuality in the new age of mankind as channeled in ENTHUSIASM. This means exceptional projection of self into the administration and expansion of the broader modern potentials. The transit occurs about every eighty-four years or perhaps once in a lifetime. If he is able to establish himself significantly in some important development of the new order in daily activity, he may know that he is fulfilling himself most uniquely. If Uranus, in the rare possibility of it, is also stationary at the moment, the indication is dramatically strengthened.

TRANSITING URANUS, passing over the zodiacal sign and degree occupied by SATURN AT BIRTH, indicates the native's heightened individuality in the new age of mankind as channeled in SENSITIVENESS. This means unusual awareness of the particular modern factors of life now embodied in established everyday routine. The transit occurs about every eighty-four years or perhaps once in a lifetime. If he is able to develop these factors more significantly at some crucial point in current affairs, he may know he is functioning in a high destiny. If Uranus, in the rare possibility of it, is also stationary at the moment, the indication is definitely intensified.

TRANSITING URANUS, passing over the zodiacal sign and degree occupied by URANUS AT BIRTH, indicates the native's heightened individuality in the new age of mankind as channeled in INDEPENDENCE. This means an exceptionally freewheeling manifestation of selfhood in the expanding modern pattern of everyday existence. The transit occurs about every eighty-four years or perhaps once in a lifetime. If he is able to break out of entrenched limitations in some dramatically effective fashion, he may know that he is significantly spading up new ground. If Uranus, in the rare possibility of it, is also stationary at the moment, the indication is unusually strengthened.

TRANSITING URANUS, passing over the zodiacal sign and degree occupied by NEPTUNE AT BIRTH, indicates the native's heightened individuality in the new age of mankind as channeled in OBLIGATION. This means a complete acceptance of larger responsibilities in the expanding modern pattern of everyday existence. The transit occurs about every eighty-four years or perhaps once in a lifetime. If he is able to organize significant factors of the new cooperation of human potentialities in sudden and convincing fashion, he may know he is contributing to worthwhile trends in everyday affairs. If Uranus, in the rare possibility of it, is also stationary at the moment, the indicaiton is significantly expanded.

TRANSITING URANUS, passing over the zodiacal sign and degree occupied by PLUTO AT BIRTH, indicates the native's heightened individuality in the new age of mankind as channeled in OBSESSION or total self-dedication. This means ultimate self-identification in operations that can be of supreme importance. The transit occurs about every eighty-four years or perhaps once in a lifetime. If he is able to build himself successfully into some widespread human cause through a dramatic eventuation, he may know he has probably established himself very definitely. If Uranus, in the rare possibility of it, is also stationary at this point, the indication is truly magnified.

TRANSITING URANUS, passing over the zodiacal sign and degree occupied by THE MOON AT BIRTH, indicates the native's heightened individuality in the new age of mankind as channeled in FEELING. This means emotional rehearsal of any unique development in experience. The transit occurs about every eighty-four years or perhaps once in a lifetime. If he has been able to bring something significant in crisis to this creative adjustment, he has established special validation for his procedures. If Uranus, in the rare possibility of it, is also stationary at this point, the indication is intensified.

## NASCENT RESPONSIBILITY

TRANSITING NEPTUNE, passing over the zodiacal sign and degree occupied by MERCURY AT BIRTH, indicates the native's increasing responsibility for man's welfare channeled in MENTALITY. This means exceptional realization of his broader modern potentials. The transit occurs about every one hundred and sixty-four years and so never in some lifetimes. If, at a moment of occurrence, he is able to contribute dramatically to an understanding of the new social order, he is shown to be living significantly and should be urged to continue in his course. If Neptune is stationary at this point, the indication is highly intensified.

TRANSITING NEPTUNE, passing over the zodiacal sign and degree occupied by THE SUN AT BIRTH, indicates the native's increasing responsibility for man's welfare channeled in PURPOSE. This means driving contribution to remedial ends in this field. The transit occurs about every one hundred and sixty-four years and so never in a lifetime. If, at a moment of occurrence, he is able to produce dramatic results in some given phase of effort, he is revealed as a significant figure in the area and should be given special encouragement. If Neptune is stationary at this point, the indication is particularly vital.

TRANSITING NEPTUNE, passing over the zodiacal sign and

degree occupied by VENUS AT BIRTH, indicates the native's increasing responsibility for man's welfare channeled in ACQUISITIVENESS. This means unusual rapport with things of usefulness, and capacity for commandeering them. The transit occurs about every one hundred and sixty-four years and so never in a lifetime. If, at a moment of occurrence, he is able to put many significant factors together in dramatic ameliorations, he is shown to have an importance that should have support. If Neptune is stationary at this point, the indication is greatly strengthened.

TRANSITING NEPTUNE, passing over the zodiacal sign and degree occupied by MARS AT BIRTH, indicates the native's increasing responsibilities for man's welfare channeled in INITIATIVE. This means the inauguration and continued stimulus of productive measures for social progress. The transit occurs about every one hundred and sixty-four years and so never in some lives. If, at a moment of occurrence, he is able to revivify some crucial project or service in this vital field, he is revealed as a potential pioneer in human engineering. If Neptune is stationary at this point, the indication is highly significant.

TRANSITING NEPTUNE, passing over the zodiacal sign and degree occupied by JUPITER AT BIRTH, indicates the native's increasing responsibility for man's welfare channeled in ENTHUSIASM. This means the enlistment of personality or individual motivation in the effort for social betterment. The transit occurs about every one hundred and sixty-four years and so never in some lives. If, at a moment of occurrence, he is able to step forward in vital leadership during exceptional crisis, he emerges as a figure of importance to be given all possible help. If Neptune is stationary at this point, the indication is exceptionally intensified.

TRANSITING NEPTUNE, passing over the zodiacal sign and degree occupied by SATURN AT BIRTH, indicates the native's increasing responsibility for man's welfare channeled in SENSITIVENESS. This means the necessity for common sense or wisdom in furthering the effort for social betterment. The transit occurs about every one hundred and sixty-four years and so never in some lives. If, at a moment of occurrence, he is able to get acceptance for an intelligence really encompassing some difficulty in crisis, he gains an authority that should have lasting recognition. If Neptune is stationary at this point, the indication is greatly heightened.

TRANSITING NEPTUNE, passing over the zodiacal sign and degree occupied by URANUS AT BIRTH, indicates the native's increasing responsibility for man's welfare channeled in INDEPENDENCE. This means the breaking away from the limitations of medieval society through the emancipation of the individual. The transit occurs about every one hundred and sixty-four years and so never in a lifetime. If, at a moment of occurrence, he is able to further some vital feature of this breakaway, he may gain a special position that should have solid support. If Neptune is stationary at this point, the indication has marked intensification.

Transiting Neptune, passing over the zodiacal sign and degree occupied by NEPTUNE AT BIRTH, would indicate the native's increasing responsibility for man's welfare channeled in OBLIGATION. This would mean intensive organization of the more revolutionary details of the social betterment in progress. The transit occurs about every one hundred and sixty-four years, not likely to occur in one's lifetime. If at a moment of occurrence he would be able, at some very significant juncture, to dramatize the inherent uniqueness of the eventuation, he might gain a well-established influence of great value. If Neptune is stationary at this point to help make the indication remotely possible, it would have high effectiveness.

TRANSITING NEPTUNE, passing over the zodiacal sign and degree occupied by PLUTO AT BIRTH, indicates the native's increasing responsibility for man's welfare channeled in OBSESSION. This means the ultimate special need for extraordinarily dedicated individuals to carry forward the fluid structured social order of the incoming new age of humanity. The transit occurs about every one hundred and sixty-four years and so never in a lifetime. If, at a moment of occurrence, he is able to make a significant demonstration of the needed self-dedication, he may gain high influence. If Neptune is stationary at this point, the indication has accentuated value.

TRANSITING NEPTUNE, passing over the zodiacal sign and degree occupied by THE MOON AT BIRTH, indicates the native's increasing responsibility for man's welfare channeled in FEELING. This means the need for emotion or concern in the establishment of the new social order for humanity. The transit occurs about every one hundred and sixty-four years and so never in a lifetime. If, at a moment of occurrence, he is able to make significant demonstration of the new high rapport with everyday practical circumstances, he can find a vital place for himself. If Neptune is stationary at this point, the indication will be magnified.

## NASCENT ENLIGHTENMENT

TRANSITING PLUTO, passing over the zodiacal sign and degree occupied by MERCURY AT BIRTH, indicates the native's broadening orientation in new-age potentials manifest in MENTALITY. This means an enlightened understanding that enables him to serve his fellows in true respect for their individuality. The transit occurs too infrequently for usual consideration but if it does, and he gives spectacular evidence of high insight at the time, his life can be seen to have exceptional significance. If Pluto is stationary at this point, the indication is more dramatic.

TRANSITING PLUTO, passing over the zodiacal sign and degree occupied by the SUN AT BIRTH, indicates the native's broadening orientation in new-age potentials manifest in PURPOSE. This means an enlightened ambition that enables him to serve his fellows in true respect for their individuality. The transit occurs too infrequently for usual consideration but if it does, and he gives spectacular evidence of high socioeconomic statesmanship at the time, his life is shown to have marked significance. If Pluto is stationary at this point, the indication is more exceptional.

TRANSITING PLUTO, passing over the zodiacal sign and degree occupied by VENUS AT BIRTH, indicates the native's broadening orientation in the new-age potentials manifest in ACQUISITIVENESS. This means enlightened rapport with daily realities that enables him to serve his fellows in true respect for their individuality. The transit occurs too infrequently for usual consideration but if it does, and he gives spectacular evidence of high socioeconomic appreciation at the time, his life is revealed as unusually significant. If Pluto is stationary at this point, the indication is definitely sharpened.

TRANSITING PLUTO, passing over the zodiacal sign and degree occupied by MARS AT BIRTH, indicates the native's broadening orientation in the new-age potentials manifest in INITIATIVE. This means an enlightened activation of everyday routine that enables him to serve his fellows in true respect for their individuality. The transit occurs too infrequently for usual consideration but if it does, and he gives spectacular evidence of needed sustainment for some vital project at the time, his life has real certification of its significance. If Pluto is stationary at this point, the indication is intensified.

TRANSITING PLUTO, passing over the zodiacal sign and degree occupied by JUPITER AT BIRTH, indicates the native's broadening orientation in the new-age potentials manifest in ENTHUSIASM. This means an enlightened personalizing of everyday activity that enables him to serve his fellows in true respect for their individuality. The transit occurs too infrequently for usual consideration but if it does, and he gives spectacular evidence of suddenly effective personal influence, his life is shown to have very dramatic significance. If Pluto is stationary at this point, the indication is heightened.

TRANSITING PLUTO, passing over the zodiacal sign and degree occupied by SATURN AT BIRTH, indicates the native's broadening orientation in the new-age potentials manifest in SENSITIVENESS. This means an enlightened intellectual capacity that enables him to serve his fellows in true respect for their individuality. The transit occurs too infrequently for usual consideration but if it does, and he gives spectacular evidence of suddenly effective analysis in some major crisis of human affairs, his life has vital demonstration of its significance. If Pluto is stationary at this point, the indication is magnified.

TRANSITING PLUTO, passing over the zodiacal sign and degree occupied by URANUS AT BIRTH, indicates the native's broadening orientation in the new-age potentials manifest in INDEPENDENCE. This means an enlightened self-liberation that enables him to serve his fellows in true respect for their individuality. The transit occurs too infrequently for usual consideration but if it does, and he gives spectacular evidence of competence that turns the tide of events to successful culminations, his life is revealed in its real significance. If Pluto is stationary at this point, the indication is greatly sharpened.

TRANSITING PLUTO, passing over the zodiacal sign and degree occupied by NEPTUNE AT BIRTH, indicates the native's broadening orientation in the new-age potentials manifest in OBLIGATION. This means an enlightened self-enlistment in vital responsibilities that enables him to serve his fellows in true respect for their individuality. The transit occurs too infrequently for usual consideration but if it does, and he gives spectacular evidence of ability to hold all things together successfully, his life is shown significant indeed. If Pluto is stationary at this point, the indication can be very dramatic.

TRANSITING PLUTO cannot except in infancy pass over the zodiacal sign and degree occupied by PLUTO AT BIRTH, or the opposite sign and degree in any lifetime.

TRANSITING PLUTO, passing over the zodiacal sign and degree occupied by THE MOON AT BIRTH, indicates the native's broadening orientation in the new-age potentials manifest in FEELING or in common rapport with everyday pertinences of conscious existence. This means the practical enrichment of experience through emotional activation. The transit occurs too infrequently for usual consideration but if it does, and he moves in dramatic concern over important conditions needlessly fragmented, his life can be seen to be truly significant. If Pluto is stationary at this point, the indication is intensified.

## NATURAL INVOLVEMENT

THE TRANSITING MOON, passing over the zodiacal sign and degree occupied by MERCURY AT BIRTH, indicates a possible stimulation of the native's MENTALITY in connection with the natural involvement in which he rehearses his experience through his emotions. This means simple realization. The transit happens each lunar month and, if there is significant acceptance in mind of the bare facts of some important situation, there is demonstration of his ability to face up to life's actualities. If not, there may be a need for warning against prejudice.

The moon has no stations, and the lunar eclipse has only very minor significance.

THE TRANSITING MOON, passing over the zodiacal sign and degree occupied by THE SUN AT BIRTH, indicates a possible stimulation of the native's PURPOSE in connection with the natural involvement in which he rehearses his experience through his emotions. This means simple restlessness. The transit happens each lunar month and, if there is significant decisiveness in dealing with the bare facts of some important situation, there is demonstration of his capacity to hold to his course. If not, there may be a need for warning against vacillation.

THE TRANSITING MOON, passing over the zodiacal sign and degree occupied by VENUS AT BIRTH, indicates a possible stimulation of the native's ACQUISITIVENESS in connection with the natural involvement in which he rehearses his experience through his emotions. This means a simple self-interest. The transit happens each lunar month and, if there is significant possessiveness in dealing with the bare facts of some important situation, there is dramatic demonstration of his ability to preserve some essential value in things. If not, there may be a need for a warning against slovenliness.

THE TRANSITING MOON, passing over the zodiacal sign and degree occupied by MARS AT BIRTH, indicates a possible stimulation of the native's INITIATIVE in connection with the natural involvement in which he rehearses his experience through his emotions. This means simple self-expression. The transit happens each lunar month and, if there is significant continuing activity in handling the basic factors of some important situation, there is demonstration of his ability to maintain the practical operation of things. If not, there may be a need for a warning against negligence.

THE TRANSITING MOON, passing over the zodiacal sign and degree occupied by JUPITER AT BIRTH, indicates a possible stimulation of the native's ENTHUSIASM in connection with the natural involvement in which he rehearses his experience through his emotions. This means simple personality. The transit happens each lunar month and, if there is significant spirit in handling the basic factors of some important situation, there is demonstration of his ability to provide life's operations with a genuine morale. If not, there may be a need for a warning against pretentiousness.

THE TRANSITING MOON, passing over the zodiacal sign and degree occupied by SATURN AT BIRTH, indicates a possible stimulation of the native's SENSITIVENESS in connection with the natural involvement in which he rehearses his experience through his emotions. This means simple common sense. The transit happens each lunar month and, if there is significant astuteness in handling the basic factors of some important situation, there is demonstration of his capacity to provide life's operations with sound direction. If not, there may be a need for a warning against naiveté.

THE TRANSITING MOON, passing over the zodiacal sign and degree occupied by URANUS AT BIRTH, indicates a possible stimulation of the native's INDEPENDENCE in connection with the natural involvement in which he rehearses his experience through his emotions. This means exceptional resourcefulness. The transit happens each lunar month and, if there is unusually significant skill in handling some particularly new-age factors in a given situation, there is demonstration of his ability to further the new dimensions of human activity. If not, there may be a need for a warning against presumptuousness.

THE TRANSITING MOON, passing over the zodiacal sign and degree occupied by NEPTUNE AT BIRTH, indicates a possible stimulation of the native's OBLIGATION in connection with the natural involvement in which he rehearses his experience through his emotions. This means exceptional reliability. The transit happens each lunar month and, if there is unusually significant group perspective in handling particular new-age factors in a given situation, there is demonstration of his capacity to organize the greater scope of human living. If not, there may be a need for a warning against social insensitivity.

THE TRANSITING MOON, passing over the zodiacal sign and degree occupied by PLUTO AT BIRTH, indicates a possible stimulation of the native's OBSESSION in connection with the natural involvement in which he rehearses his experience through his emotions. This means exceptionally total self-dedication. The transit happens each lunar month and, if there is remarkably personal and successful handling of particularly new-age factors in a given situaiton, there is demonstration of his potentially great stature. If not, there may be a need for a warning against megalomania.

THE TRANSITING MOON, passing over the zodiacal sign and degree occupied by THE MOON AT BIRTH, indicates a possible stimulation of the native's FEELING in connection with the natural involvement in which he rehearses his experience through his emotions. In crisis this means simple temperament. The transit happens each lunar month and, if there is significant sincerity in dealing with the bare facts of some important situation, there is demonstration of his ability to hold to his moral standards. If not, there may be a need for a warning against instability.

# PART IV

## *PRACTICAL APPPLICATIONS*

# Chapter Seven

## *THE WATERGATE SCANDAL*

The author of an astrological textbook faces a major difficulty when selecting example cases. They must certainly be based on reliable data, and must have definite relevance to the specific technical points they are chosen to illustrate, and must best serve his reader to understand the points being put forth. The example should provide one or more instances of a widely known person or episode. It should also be some actuality about which there is an overall concensus of judgment and in this way take advantage of the familiarity and reasonable access to available detailed, pertinent information. The example should be one of strong common interest, not likely to wane in too short a time so that the book will not become outdated too quickly, and have its value consequently depreciated. An event that meets these criteria is the Watergate scandal, unquestionably an utterly devastating punctuation in the political history of the United States. Obviously, there is very little chance of this stark, dramatic epitome of moral corruption in public life ever being entirely forgotten because of its exceptionally ramifying features. It has eclipsed the infamous Tweed Ring and the Teapot Dome skulduggery by its far deeper and more insidious challenge to human honor and decency.

To instrument the case of Watergate as this basic example, I will generally apply the astrological technique of planetary surrogation, the tested validity of which has been demonstrated by long customary tradition though, perhaps, not too familiar to the casual student. The technique has proven impeccable in almost endless instances. The conception originally was that the personal horoscope of the royal ruler of a given land became the effective chart of the national destiny. Now, astrologers have made a practical adaption of that principle and found that the individual nativity of the actual administrative executive of any political (or business) organization will accurately provide an effective horoscope for such a group, regardless of size, as long as the power remains vested in that same incumbent individual. Consequently, the application of personal astrology techniques already presented in this text will be brought to climactic illustration with the analysis of the transits relevant to the birth chart of former President Richard M. Nixon during this crucial period, who by his deliberate acts was entirely responsible for his own downfall.

## THE GREATER CYCLES

An illustrative interpretation of the Watergate scandal should methodically start with the indications of the slower, most outlying planets, in the order of their distance from the sun. Relating them, in turn, according to the zodiacal sign containing them at the time of the events.

PLUTO entered Libra in October of 1971 only to return to Virgo in April of 1972 for three months and then reenter Libra to stay until November of 1983. The arrest of five men attempting to fix wiretap equipment for bugging the national headquarters of the Democratic Party in the Watergate office building at Washington occurred on June 17 in 1972, and the fact that this occurred when the planet was back in Virgo suggests the ultimately relative unimportance of this one of the number of petty criminal acts in contrast with the major event of President Nixon's great lie. There was far more involved than an incident of ill luck of unhappy consequence in the life of an individual obsessed with the dubious morality and all too frequent expediency in the power struggle of American politics.

Pluto's passage through the sign Libra marks a special emphasis of OBSESSION in EQUIVALENCE and this suggests first of all a vital pivoting of history on the acts of individuals of unimpeachable stubbornness of spirit. Libra, in its leveling-off or balancing potential, identifies the overall necessity for preserving the genius of American democracy for the incoming new great Aquarian Age. This would mean restoring the governmental structure of three independent departments, or striking down the almost absolute power of the presidency coming to its climax with the curiously sealed-in White House cabal. With dramatic staunchness, brought by circumstances to confrontation with the national concern, was the unwavering concern and effective court procedures of such figures as Federal Judge John J. Sirica. It is only in this overall context that Watergate can be understood. Thus a concomitant epochal calling to ultimate ethical account of key individuals in high places, shown by astrology to have exceptional accentuation in this Pluto period, is provided in the tragedy of Vice President Spiro Agnew. On August 6 in 1973 he announced that he was under investigation in his home state for accepting bribes while he was governor and indeed was continuing to receive them. He resigned in disgrace on October 10.

On the world stage there is far more vital eventuation, in what conveniently, if awkwardly, could be seen as an expanded sort of global Watergate. On the whole it can be taken more on the immediately positive side. The precipitation of events here was the shrewd course of President Anwar Sadat of Egypt, who veered away from what was becoming an unpalatable union of his country with a Libya under tight control by the Muslim fanatic Muammar-al Qaddafi and instead forged a new Arab axis with the exceptionally able King Faisal of Saudi Arabia in September of 1973, and who thereupon, on October 6, opened in partnership with Syria his successfully surprise attack on Israel in the short Yom Kippur War. While the Israelis turned this into a military victory, but otherwise a hopelessly Pyrrhic one, the Arabian world in a new found morale promptly established the phenomenal increases in the price of oil and brought about the complete upset of the long-established financial hegemony of the Western Industrial nations. This is a fresh foundation on which history is being written, and which the astrologer should understand well if he wishes to resort to the mundane branch of his art. The layman, of course, can be given at least a reliable summary for general orientation.

NEPTUNE entered Sagittarius initially on January 4 of 1970 but went back into Scorpio May 3 in retrogradation and then returned to the new sign on November 6 for its uninterrupted stay of some thirteen years. Thus what embraces the general period of Watergate is here an astrological proposition of OBLIGATION in ADMINISTRATION. The official actions of Richard Nixon conveniently epitomized the current surging of humanity in the unfolding national destiny for better or worse, and the tragic swing of the pendulum toward the latter can be identified through the significant detail. The President in his state-of-the Union message on January 22 in 1970 stated that his major and immediate goal in foreign policy was to end the Vietnam war and on April 20 he announced that an additional 150,000 troops would be brought home by the following spring. Yet, with May, he had made the brief invasion of neutral Cambodia that precipitated violent protest against the high-handed governmental procedures.

Dissatisfaction was widespread, and there was no real attempt to meet it. A demonstration in this year on May 4 led to the reckless killing of four students at Kent State University in Ohio. Walter Hickel, who was Secretary of the Interior and the sole cabinet member daring to speak up against presidential policies during the height of the campus unrest, was dismissed on November 25. A few details of mundane astrology might help the layman's perspective at this point, since a prior emphasis of the sign Libra came to special prominence in a preceding Neptune cycle. This was when that planet's entrance into the sign to stay for thirteen-odd years corresponded very closely to the achievement of a controlled release of atomic energy, or what was certainly a key event in the inauguration of the new great age for mankind. Mastery of the atom was unquestionably an epochal leveling-off in general understanding, through taking the individual into unknown depths of reality. In rough terms, everybody born 1942 through 1956 has his natal Neptune placed in Libra, to give him a character such as calls him in these days to the task of clearing away what has least value and of re-establishing what retains value in balance through perhaps every area of effort. In 1970 the youth of the land, ranging from fourteen to twenty-eight in age, were approaching the full tide of their generation and its opportunity to begin to take over the course of life for almost everybody in one significant way or another. In a context of obligation in leadership as well as everything else, there was apparently in 1970 not the least effort by the prominent men in authority to include their younger compeers in any of the vital administrative details of mankind's transition. They themselves had little sense of the new order of socio-economic or political life. Here was the seed of the growing violence and intensification of the moment. Indeed, by astrological indications it may continue at least in general terms until the threshold of the 1980's.

URANUS entered Libra initially on September 28 in 1968 but from May 1 until June 24 of the next year it was retrograding back into and out of Virgo again. Richard Nixon, however, had been elected on November 5, or immediately after the planet's first ingress into the sign of swing to significant balance, which was coming to its historic importance in modern times at this point. His success at the polls became one of the most spectacular comebacks in American history, even if by the very slimmest of margins. This gave him potential stature in an epochal context, and here was exceptional opportunity in connection with the actual transition of the whole globe into the new Aquarian Age. His initial election was a manifestation of INDEPENDENCE in EQUIVALENCE. His was the chance to play a dominant and a wonderfully successful role in advancing the American form of democracy throughout the world at large. Nobody before or since could possibly have been in a position to promote or execute a foundational alignment of some more peaceful or enduring sort between the two great Communistic giants through the intrinsically greater power of resources of the third and democratic superstate. The grounds for this were his remarkably unconditioned 1972 visits to China in late February and to the Soviet Union in late May. This was before the campaign illegalities that completely changed the overall tide of things, and gradually built up the great sweep of them that ultimately toppled him from his remarkable height.

The debacle of course would be under the same indications that had charted his rise. In afterview it can be seen that his extraordinary buffeting by life in so many respects had made the independence of this indication a personal need, rather than the almost cosmic opportunity that had come to him. The poison of peership with power created the fear of losing it, and his equivalence degenerated to his panic for its preservation. This would account for the tragic errors, as the creation of the Committee to Re-Elect the President in order to bypass the regular Republican organization.

SATURN entered Gemini on June 18 in 1971, but slipped back into Taurus by retrogradation on January 10 in 1972 and did not re-enter Gemini to complete the former full cycle until February 21 in the new year. This later date finally established the new cycle of SENSITIVENESS in VIVIFICATION, or a time of probable quickening of events to particular significance. It has striking correspondence to the public assurance by President Nixon on June 22 that "There is no involvement by the White House" in the Watergate break-in. This apparently had sufficient importance to him to lead him to reaffirm on August 29 that "no one on the White House staff . . . was involved in this very bizarre incident." Here is strange if unwitting acceptance of Plato's suggestion in his *Republic* that the masses cannot grasp ultimate realization, and that in consequence political leadership must make use of a magnificent lie (as Jowett translates the Greek) or what has been oversimplified in the notion that whatever is endlessly affirmed will at length be believed more or less by everybody.

It has been pointed out that only most superficially can the bungled attempt to wiretap the Democratic national headquarters be taken as the actual beginning of the great scandal. It could be true, in Benjamin Franklin's words, that for want of a nail a shoe was lost and then a horse and then a rider and then a battle and finally a kingdom was lost. But could a lack of such a nail ever predict so horrendous a result. Even astrology cannot with any accuracy predict matters more than one stage ahead of its immediate conditions. Even horoscopic progressions must be charted in a definitive context for any dependable suggestiveness. Nixon was destroyed in his splendid potentials by a wrong choice of context at a vitally critical moment in his career. Saturn has long and traditionally been the great disciplinarian of mankind in its identification with the gaining and possessing of wisdom and this, as an awareness of pertinence or a proper appreciation of any and all experience. His deliberate employment of this capacity for a bringing of things to life in attempting to enthrone falsehood as truth, was a perversion of human decency or moral courage. But no less it was still a dramatic demonstration of the astrological potentiality.

JUPITER was in Capricorn when events came to their Watergate, both at the time of the original break-in at the Democratic headquarters and at the time of Richard Nixon's magnificent lie. Here the manifestation of pivotal personality in the great scandal can be seen to have been the fruit of a proposition of ENTHUSIASM in DISCRIMINATION. The President had a splendid opportunity to demonstrate the reality of his ceaseless announcement of devotion to law and order by throwing everything wide open to investigation at the start and, as he did at the end with his resignation, freely admitting his own mistake. He could perhaps have become the popular hero in really facing the superficially ridiculous—but widespread serious—consequences of the re-election irregularities. Instead he reasoned himself into greater and greater dimensions of error, and thereupon became almost the hapless architect of his own downfall.

THE SUN was in Gemini at the time of the arrest of the political plumbers, to indicate PURPOSE in VIVIFICATION and this suggests the exceptional effort to get special or inside information concerning Democratic strategy and perhaps detailed campaign plans. The miscarriage was the result of an extraordinary carelessness in taping a lock open and in the manner of doing it. The sun was moving into the sign Cancer when the first statement of Nixon's magnificent lie was made, and indeed was almost precisely on the new cusp to suggest perhaps unusual manifestation of PURPOSE in EXPANSION. The rapid spreading of the significance, in its ill-conceived purpose, simply backfired. The result was reversed hope and expectation.

## THE PLANETARY HOURS

To have an adequate example of the planetary hours would always be difficult in matters of any importance. Even sure dates are hard to obtain in developments of general concern, and to have precise minutes would of course be virtually impossible most of the time. To have something for the investigator, however, the time was taken for the exact moment it came to the writing of these lines in the rough-draft or original unedited manuscript of this text. This was 7:39 a.m. mean local time on Thursday March 27, 1975, six miles east of Stanwood, Washington at latitude 48°15' north. This was a Mars hour at latitude 50° north, extending from 7:02 to 8:03 in the latter half of the month. This is an hour regarded as best for starting things, or continually keeping them in motion, and thus it was encouragement to hold to the task in this project. Here was a measure of very considerable pioneering effort to expand the use of the transits in everyday life, and on a strictly psychological or personal basis.

This was an example of horary astrology, a quite popular branch of the horoscopic art and often of the greatest value in right-down-to-earth matters. It does not have the reliability of the basic natal astrology, or the other branches grounded in life and natural phenomena and their progressive unfoldment. It does best in skillful hands, when there is no effort to get sound guidance for things of importance out of trivial thought and impulses, but it is far closer to intuitive insight than the more definitively scientific procedures.

## THE SHORTER CYCLES

MARS was in Cancer at the time of the Watergate arrests and Nixon's magnificent lie and the dominating factor of indication is here shown as a repeated proposition of INITIATIVE in EXPANSION or testimony to the highly dramatic spread of the general concern over the scandal that before too long would exhibit an unstoppable pyramiding. In time just about the whole of the government functions in Washington were involved. Here was testimony, if not to be recognized until perhaps much later, that the die had indeed been cast for the country's self-blinded chief executive.

VENUS was in Gemini when the great scandal had its superficial or immediate origins, the sign into which it had just retrograded for a species of gestation before moving ahead expansively in Cancer with early August, and this zodiacal punctuation showed the untoward circumstances to be a proposition of ACQUISITIVENESS in the highly accentuated VIVIFICATION. There would be the unlimited and almost consistently illegal employment of any and all resources of the government, as well as of the extraordinary collection, if not virtual conscription of, campaign funds, for the most part not only to re-elect the President but more and more to protect the tight little White House clique.

MERCURY was in Cancer at the time of the events precipitating the Watergate eventuations, which revealed the overall possible manifestation of national morale or aplomb at a historical moment of such dramatic opportunity for an American president. With the underlying potentiality shown here to be a proposition of MENTALITY in EXPANSION, there could be the almost illimitable self-conviction of a human mind in its unbroken course. Its particular slanting could continue most consistently, no matter how wrong this might be by any standard.

THE MOON was in Virgo when the Watergate arrests took place and this shows that in overall public context the event was a proposition of FEELING in ASSIMILATION, or perhaps a coming to crucial fullness of potentiality in the efforts of the Committee to Re-elect the President. Organized to supplant the Republican National Committee, it pre-empted a special privacy and freedom of action wholly its own. Richard Nixon might have felt this a chance to assimilate himself more thoroughly into the substance of the American people however in eventuation it came to be dramatized. It quite easily resulted in something very much the reverse of what he had anticipated. The moon was in Scorpio when the magnificent lie was first affirmed, and this identifies that more important step as a proposition of FEELING in CREATIVITY or certainly an example of unfettered choice and the utterly impulsive self-mobilization that under more constructive circumstances could have furthered the epochal contribution that somehow never got in motion. There was no capitalization on the dramatic moment of rapprochment with Peking and Moscow.

# CHAPTER EIGHT
## *THE EXAMPLE HOROSCOPE*

Even when a very well known individual is selected for the example horoscope in an astrological text, there may be some readers for whom a thumbnail sketch is helpful. Richard Milhous Nixon was born in a small town a short distance from Anaheim in California. His were typical self-sufficient middle-class circumstances. He had normal good education with thorough professional legal training that culminated in graduation with honors from Duke University. He served in the navy, and had an apprenticeship in politics through nearly two full terms as congressman in Washington D.C. Gaining distinction through an exaggerated anti-Communism, he won a landslide victory in election to the Senate in 1950 and in 1952 gained the number two spot on the Republican ticket with General Dwight Eisenhower. It was then that his first scandal broke with the discovery of his secret slush fund, but he went on television and was successful in toughening it out and gaining election as vice-president in 1952. Receiving the Republican nomination for president in 1960, he was defeated narrowly by John F. Kennedy. In another two years he had a decidedly humiliating loss in the California race for governor, and apparently was passing into oblivion. Thanks, however, to dogged, intensified behind-the-scenes building up his Republican bridges, he won the presidential nomination again in 1968 and edged into the White House by an exceedingly narrow margin. His landslide re-election in 1972 ushered in the ultimate collapse of what had been close to superlative achievement.

## NIXON'S CHART

The use of transits in the dynamic astrology, as a significant buttressing for the progressions of the natal horoscope,

## NIXON'S CHART

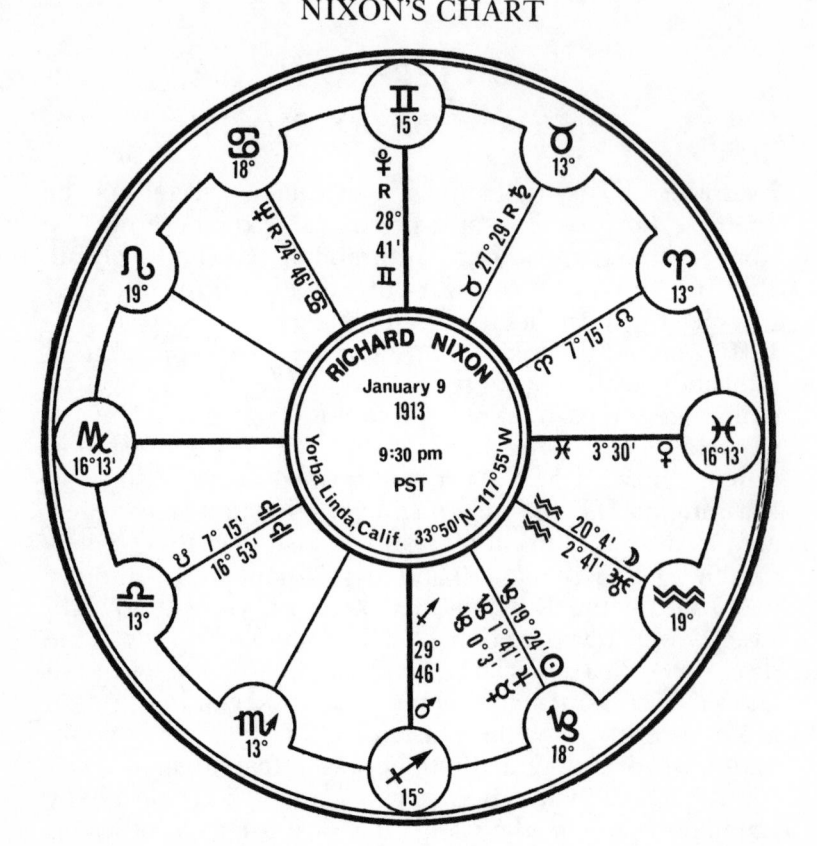

is often carried into a minutia of detail that can soon be self-defeating through the little possible importance of the indication and a parallel loss of reliability. What seems to be the most effective technique in this area is to limit attention to the solar eclipses of the lights and the stations of the eight planets that in astrological perspective can have retrograde motion and to take nothing but conjunction and opposition into account. This of course has been the procedure followed through the earlier pages of the present text. In the Watergate era of the luckless Nixon career, there are ten transiting indications to be taken as significantly relevant.

SOLAR ECLIPSE IN CAPRICORN DIRECTLY OPPOSITE PRESIDENT NIXON'S NATAL NEPTUNE IN THE ZODIAC WITHIN A 39′ ORB OF EXACTNESS, JANUARY 16, 1972. This indication of the strengthening or heightening of his OBLIGATION through his overall vitality as a proposition of his functioning DISCRIMINATION corresponds to the fundamental choices he was making in his almost frantic outreach toward success in this repeat trip to the national polls, following the narrow squeak of his victory four years previously. Unhappily he chose to build on close-in ties to himself rather than taking advantage of the unfolding achievement that was his major opportunity, and so significantly bypassed the Republican National Committee in establishing early in that year the Committee to Re-elect the President or the rather covert body that in due course would instrument his debacle. Almost immediately after his dramatic visits to Peking and Moscow he first (and at that point perhaps spontaneously) made the initial statement of the magnificent lie and thus at core raised the spector of his greatest weakness or his tendency to override crisis by the sheer arrogance that had been successful only by a hair's breadth in the Eisenhower campaign of 1952.

SOLAR ECLIPSE IN CANCER DIRECTLY OPPOSITE PRESIDENT NIXON'S NATAL SUN WITHIN A 42′ ORB, JULY 10, 1972. This indication of the strengthening or heightening of his PURPOSE in self-drive through his overall vitality as a proposition of his functioning EXPANSION corresponds to the building results of his achievements in foreign relations at the best but more enduringly and at the worst to his deliberate and so increasingly significant repetition of the magnificent lie on August 29. Here is astrological testimony to the cancerous growth potential of the Watergate scandal.

TRANSITING JUPITER STATIONARY GOING DIRECT IN SAGITTARIUS OPPOSITE PRESIDENT NIXON'S NATAL PLUTO WITHIN A 12′ ORB, AUGUST 25, 1972. This indication of a possible stimulation of his OBSESSION through functioning potentials of ENTHUSIASM in ADMINISTRATION corresponds more definitely to the magnificent lie as now particularly characteristic of his personality or tendency to throw the whole of himself into everything he did, but quite on his own terms. Here is astrological testimony to his capacity to plunge ahead in any course with, at the worst, no great concern over the means employed.

TRANSITING MERCURY STATIONARY GOING RETROGRADE IN LEO OPPOSITE PRESIDENT NIXON'S NATAL URANUS WITHIN A 40' ORB, July 6, 1973. This indication of a possible stimulation of his INDEPENDENCE through functioning potentials of MENTALITY in ASSURANCE corresponds to the discovery that all conversations in his White House office were automatically recorded on tape, and the start on July 23 of Special Prosecutor Archibald Cox's effort to get access to these. Here is astrological identification of the very real threat to Nixon's cover-up when it could have been high challenge to further genuine achievement.

TRANSITING JUPITER STATIONARY GOING DIRECT IN AQUARIUS ON THE PLACE OF PRESIDENT NIXON'S NATAL URANUS WITHIN A 24' ORB, SEPTEMBER 28, 1973. This indication of a possible stimulation of his INDEPENDENCE through functioning potentials of ENTHUSIASM in LOYALTY corresponds to the neat little scheme worked out to block the ultimate net that Special Prosecutor Cox was weaving about him on the basis of the White House tapes. Bringing in Senator John Stennis as probably unwittingly accessory, to certify the correctness of special transcripts of new vital reels so that they themselves would not have to be surrendered under subpoena, the arrangement identified as a compromise was offered on October 19. Here is astrological testimony to the stubborn strength of the President's faithfulness to his ends, however expressed in the worst of all possible ways.

TRANSITING MERCURY STATIONARY GOING RETROGRADE IN SCORPIO OPPOSITE PRESIDENT NIXON'S NATAL SATURN WITHIN A 53' ORB, OCTOBER 30, 1973. This indication of a possible stimulation of his SENSITIVENESS through functioning potentials of MENTALITY in CREATIVITY corresponds to what came to be known as the Saturday night massacre of the 20th or his order to discharge Special Prosecutor Cox for refusal to abide by the so-called compromise of the 19th and the fact that both his attorney-general and assistant attorney-general declined to execute it but instead promptly resigned. This pre-emptory move in complete disregard of his understanding with Congress, as obviously a step at least toward dictatorship, sent an immediate shock wave across the country and cost him a large part of the public support he had held up to this point. Here is astrological testimony to the capacity of any genuine obsession or total self-centeredness to be challengingly aware of any threat to itself, and of no less destructive than constructive nature in possible consequences.

SOLAR ECLIPSE IN CAPRICORN ON THE PLACE OF PRESIDENT NIXON'S NATAL JUPITER WITHIN A 56′ ORB, DECEMBER 24, 1973. This indication of the strengthening or heightening of his ENTHUSIASM through his overall vitality as a proposition of his functioning DISCRIMINATION corresponds to his subsequent intellectual sort of guerilla struggle with Congress as in the inescapable necessity of a new appointment with a fresh promise of an absolute free hand on November 1 of Special Prosecutor Leon Jaworski, and also by November 21 to a fresh revelation of unexplainable accidents in connection with the White House tapes and thus building to his probable realization of an even greater need for additional effort to escape from his entrapment. Here is astrological testimony to the zest in self-continuance that can contribute as much to wrong as to right ends in the personal activities of the moment.

TRANSITING SATURN STATIONARY GOING DIRECT IN GEMINI ON THE PLACE OF PRESIDENT NIXON'S NATAL PLUTO WITHIN A 54′ ORB, FEBRUARY 7, 1974. This indication of a possible stimulation of his OBSESSION through functioning potentials of SENSITIVENESS in VIVIFICATION corresponds to the grand jury indictment on March 1 of three of his very closest former associates together with four lesser individuals in the campaign illegalities. He was included, but only by intimation rather than naming him, since there was the question whether a president could be indicted. Here is astrological testimony to the ultimate weight and viability of custom and long-established order in human society, or what persists more at roof in the fundamentally inherent self-dedication to this of the average individual.

SOLAR ECLIPSE IN GEMINI ON THE PLACE OF PRESIDENT NIXON'S NATAL PLUTO WITHIN A CLOSE 11′ ORB, JUNE 20, 1974. This indication of the strengthening or heightening of his OBSESSION through his overall vitality as a proposition of his functioning VIVIFICATION corresponds to the decision of the United States Supreme Court announced on July 24 denying him executive privilege in refusing to release any White House tapes that might be vital evidence in connection with criminal activities and thereupon completely disarming him. Here is astrological testimony, by the very highest authority to the contrary otherwise, and revealing what might have been perhaps some truly magnificent opportunity for Richard Nixon rather than for the circumstances that brought him down.

TRANSITING SATURN STATIONARY GOING RETROGRADE IN CANCER OPPOSITE THE NATAL PLACE OF PRESIDENT NIXON'S SUN WITHIN A 30′ ORB, OCTOBER 31, 1974. This indication of a possible stimulation of his PURPOSE through functioning potentials óf SENSITIVENESS in EXPANSION corresponds to the tragic and dramatic denouement of the Watergate scandal in its primary lineaments with his resignation well ahead of the indication on August 8 and the complete pardon given him on September 8 by President Gerald Ford, wittingly or otherwise clearing the national arena as far as possible for a desperately needed return to full concern over its everyday course. Here, astrologically and by surrogation, was the departing gift of Richard Nixon to the nation, or the suddenly speeded-up release of the nation's overpowering tensions once and for all in this historical chapter.

There is a surface irregularity in mundane astrology, or the branch dealing with broad public affairs, that is very puzzling at times to the amateur and distressing to the fortuneteller. This is the matter of time orb, in contrast with the space orb or closeness to exactness of planetary aspects. With the vast complex of variables in a human society, it is only possible to recognize correspondences between almost arbitrarily selected lines of significances on the astrological and factual sides of reality. A horoscopic trend in January may shed light on a life trend in February or March, and so on. But it is only real distinction of the one sort that reliably illuminates the particularly emphasized nature of the other. Transmission of meaning or relevance is by no necessity a matter of simultaneousness.

# INDEX

# More books on astrology

## by Marc Edmund Jones

### A GUIDE TO HOROSCOPE INTERPRETATION

*The "whole" view of a horoscope using
planetary patterns*

## by C. E. O. Carter

### THE PRINCIPLES OF ASTROLOGY

*A clear, concise presentation of modern astrology
permeated by the author's spiritual approach*

### THE ASTROLOGY OF ACCIDENTS

*A valuable compilation of accident-horoscopes*

### AN ENCYCLOPEDIA OF PSYCHOLOGICAL ASTROLOGY

*Observations on the astrological characteristics
of about fifty diseases plus an introductory essay
on the zodiacal signs*

### THE ZODIAC AND THE SOUL

*". . . man exists in an intermediate condition, turning
his face Janus like, in two directions"—to the
material and to the heavens*

## by Isabelle M. Pagan

### FROM PIONEER TO POET, the Signs of the Zodiac Analysed

*A world renowned classic rendering a detailed
description of the characteristics of the zodiacal
signs (including specimen horoscopes)*

Available from

## QUEST BOOKS

306 W. Geneva Road, Wheaton, Ill. 60187